Advance Praise

This is a gorgeous book. It is a pleasure to read—scholarly, accessible and beautifully written. Every neophyte researcher should read this book as well as every experienced qualitative researcher, for the clarity with which the multiple, intersecting and entangled concepts and practices that affect qualitative research today are laid out, and then put to work. This book takes research methods beyond prescriptive, pre-conceived ideas about how data should be collected and analysed, embracing method as open-ended experimentation. Data, concepts and method are fluid, and in motion, concepts and life coincide, and ethics is emergent in the relationality of the research encounters. Here, researcher and participants encounter each other, affecting each other and being affected, working together on the task of making sense of the machinic assemblages, and the complex and surprising lines of force, through which lives are generated.

–Bronwyn Davies, Emeritus Professor
Western Sydney University, Australia

Exploring Data Production in Motion is a deftly written, deeply theorized exemplar of feminist poststructuralist inquiry. For qualitative researchers with even a little curiosity about inquiry in and with post-perspectives, Teija Rantala's book is a must read. It is the 'mother' of all mentor texts, first brilliantly and accessibly laying the (fluid) theoretical foundation for an inquiry in motion and then demonstrating it with her remarkable dissertation study of conservative religious women in Finland. It is a powerful teaching tool on how to think through and embrace fluid methodology inspired by poststructural theory while remaining committed to the anti-oppressive aims of critical social inquiry.

–Dr. Jennifer R. Wolgemuth
University of South Florida, US

Exploring Data Production in Motion makes a significant and timely contribution to the field of qualitative research. As a bold and innovative book, it is an energizing delight to read. This book eloquently argues for fluid feminist poststructuralist methodologies in qualitative research by creating experimental and innovative approaches to collecting and analyzing data. Fluid methodologies enable examining shifting processes, movements, intensities and affects by acknowledging the multiplicity of changing elements of inquiry. Rantala's book fabricates fresh and novel ways of doing qualitative research where disturbances and irruptions are welcomed as possibilities in order to pave the way for transformation in the affirmative ethics of inquiry. This fascinating book is warmly recommended to anyone interested in ethics and politics of qualitative research methodologies.

–Dr. Taru Leppänen, Senior Lecturer of Gender Studies
University of Turku, Finland

Exploring Data Production in Motion: Fluidity and Feminist Poststructuralism is a very special book. Fluidity in methodology beautifully weaves together critical social inquiry with poststructuralist feminist thinking. The result is a stunning piece of work which is carefully and ethically teasing out the fluidity of methodology in social research and working with the notion of multiple in qualitative inquiry. This is a highly original piece, and an important publication, that merges current research thinking with the flow and performances of becoming. The section 'future possibilities and challenges of fluid methodologies in critical social research' demonstrates how this book acts as a tour-de-force of cutting edge critical qualitative thinking, that creates new possibilities and the potential for re-conceptualising the limits and boundaries of critical social research methodology.
       –*Dr. Marek Tesar, University of Auckland, New Zealand*

This book sensitively weaves together feminist post-structuralist theory, methods and analysis employing Deleuze and Guattari's schizoanalytic cartographies to reveal the situated but also fluid nature of social qualitative inquiry. Experimenting with fluid approaches to methodology including collective open-ended methods of memory work and collaborative writing, Teija traces processes of the Conservative Laestadian women in Finland as they explore identities as women and mothers. Her experimentation draws on concepts such as lines, desiring machines and difference to make explicit the constant variation in the women's lines while they traverse conservative and religious politics of female identity, womanhood and motherhood and to show how subjectivities are produced within and through these wider social and material constellations. Through motion in inquiry sometimes seemingly contradictory identities become possible and complementary. A thought-provoking feminist contribution reconfiguring how discourse matters, becomes materialised, in women's lives while raising questions on the ethics and boundaries of differences.
       –*Dr. Nikki Fairchild, University of Chichester, U.K.*

In this book, Rantala skillfully draws on a range of feminist poststructural, feminist post-colonial, new materialist, and posthuman thinkers and concepts to both map a theoretically-driven methodology and, through a detailed exploration of a study on processes of subjectivity formation, illustrate how this methodology might work. Rantala's methodology is an affirmative experiment of movement and flux, multiplicity, relationality, and creative difference that produces situated knowledges simultaneously part of, and accountable to, the researcher. This methodology is an enactment of a process ontology, both in terms of its espousal of a logic of becoming, in the Deleuzian sense, as well as its shift in focus from subjects to processes of inquiry. Theoretically creative with accessible explanations, Rantala's work offers a methodology well-suited to multifaceted analyses that can help us produce new ways of thinking in our increasingly complex historical moment.
    –*Dr. Kathryn Strom, Ph.D, Assistant Professor of Educational Leadership*
            California State University, East Bay, US

For Emmi, Amanda, Oona, and Pasi

Exploring Qualitative Inquiry Series
Gaile S. Cannella, Editor

Exploring Qualitative Inquiry is a subseries within The **Qualitative Inquiry: Critical Ethics, Justice, and Activism** series. The broader critical series is a collection designed to provide a cross-disciplinary overview of the use of qualitative research as an avenue for justice and critical transformative activism/action socially, environmentally, and related to more-than-human/human entanglements. This type of work often engages philosophically with emergent, and often marginalized, approaches. The subseries is a set of shorter volumes, each designed to introduce a philosophical frame, component, and/or methodology put forward by a particular critical research scholar. Upon introducing the basic perspective and frame, each volume also provides an example research study to illustrate the particular view.

Exploring Data Production in Motion by Teija Rantala (2020)
Exploring Deleuze's Philosophy of Difference by David Bright (2020)
Conducting Critical Autoethnography by Donald R. Collins (2021)

Gaile S. Cannella (EdD, University of Georgia) is an independent scholar who has served as a tenured full professor at Texas A&M University–College Station and at Arizona State University–Tempe, as well as the Velma Schmidt Endowed Chair of Education at the University of North Texas. The editor of the Qualitative Inquiry: Critical Ethics, Justice, and Activism series is interested in reviewing manuscripts and proposals for possible publication in the series. Scholars who wish to be considered should email their proposals, along with two sample chapters and current CVs, to the editor. For instructions and advice on preparing a prospectus, please refer to the Myers Education Press website at http://myersedpress.com/sites/stylus/MEP/Docs/Prospectus%20Guidelines%20MEP.pdf. You can send your material to:

Gaile S. Cannella
gaile.cannella@gmail.com

EXPLORING DATA PRODUCTION IN MOTION

Fluidity and Feminist Poststructuralism

Copyright © 2020 | Myers Education Press, LLC

Published by Myers Education Press, LLC
P.O. Box 424
Gorham, ME 04038

All rights reserved. No part of this book may be reprinted or reproduced in any form or by any electronic, mechanical, or other means, now known or hereafter invented, including photocopying, recording, and information storage and retrieval, without permission in writing from the publisher.

Myers Education Press is an academic publisher specializing in books, e-books, and digital content in the field of education. All of our books are subjected to a rigorous peer review process and produced in compliance with the standards of the Council on Library and Information Resources.

LIBRARY OF CONGRESS CATALOGING-IN-PUBLICATION DATA AVAILABLE FROM LIBRARY OF CONGRESS.

13-digit ISBN 978-1-9755-0115-0 (paperback)
13-digit ISBN 978-1-9755-0114-3 (hard cover)
13-digit ISBN 978-1-9755-0116-7 (library networkable e-edition)
13-digit ISBN 978-1-9755-0117-4 (consumer e-edition)

Printed in the United States of America.

All first editions printed on acid-free paper that meets the American National Standards Institute Z39-48 standard.

Books published by Myers Education Press may be purchased at special quantity discount rates for groups, workshops, training organizations, and classroom usage. Please call our customer service department at 1-800-232-0223 for details.

Cover design by Sophie Appel, artwork by Amanda Rantala

Visit us on the web at www.myersedpress.com to browse our complete list of titles.

EXPLORING DATA PRODUCTION IN MOTION

Fluidity and Feminist Poststructuralism

By Teija Rantala

Gorham, Maine

Contents

Illustrations	xi
Acknowledgments	xiii
Introduction	xv
References	xix

SECTION ONE: FLUID CRITICAL QUALITATIVE METHODOLOGIES

1 Motion and Fluidity in Feminist Critical Social Inquiry	3
1.1. Movement in methodology	6
1.2. Fluidity	10
1.3. "Subjects" of situated knowledges	12
References	15
2 Feminist Poststructuralist Methodologies as Escape	19
2.1. What is feminist poststructuralism?	20
2.2. Feminist writing practices	22
2.3. Memory work and collective biography	24
2.4. Collaborative data production	27
References	28

SECTION TWO: FLUID METHODOLOGIES IN SPECIFIC CONTEXTS

3 Overview of the Method	35
3.1. A brief contextualization of the study	35
3.2. The data production	38
3.3. Fluidity and movement in feminist data production	46
References	49
4 Composing Processual Analysis	53
4.1. Reading the data with concepts and theories	54
4.2. Schizoanalysis	60
References	67

5 The Movements of Lines — 71
    5.1. Flowing lines — 73
    5.2. Breaks in the flow: Relational and sexual configurations — 77
    5.3. Temporary formations — 80
    5.4. Brief summary on the lines — 86
    References — 88

SECTION THREE:
FINAL THOUGHTS ON CRITICAL RESEARCH IN MOTION

6 The Possibilities and Challenges of the Methodologies in Motion — 95
    6.1. The aftermaths of fluid feminist critical social inquiry — 97
    6.2. Some future possibilities and challenges of fluid methodologies in critical social research — 101
    References — 108

Glossary — 111
Author Bio — 115
Index — 117

Illustrations

Artwork on the cover, Amanda Rantala, 2018.

Pic. 3.1.1.   40
Photo of the handwritten autobiographical writings
(Autobiographical writings data, 2012–2013).

Pic. 3.1.2.   41
A close-up photo of a writing (Autobiographical writings data, 2012–2013).

Pic. 4.1.1.   56
Movement in the text (Autobiographical writings data, 2012–2013).

Pic. 4.1.2.   58
Intensities in the text (Autobiographical writings data, 2012–2013).

Pic. 4.2.1.   61
Aspirations in the data (Notes of the author, 21 November 2014).

Pic. 4.2.2.   62
Mapping the aspirations for analysis
(Illustration by the author, 28 November 2014).

Pic. 4.2.3.   62
Codings of a desiring machine (Illustration by the author, 8 March 2015).

Pic. 4.2.4.   63
Functions of a religious desiring machine
(Illustration by the author, 18 November 2014).

Pic. 4.2.5.   64
Picturing the stratification of lines (Deleuze & Guattari, 1987)
(Illustration by the author, 23 October 2014).

Pic. 4.2.6.   64
Smooth and striated lines in the analysis
(Notes and illustrations by the author, 29 October 2014).

Pic. 4.2.7.   65
Lines coming out of the desiring machines
(Illustration by the author, 8 March 2015).

Pic. 4.2.8.   65
Differenciation and movement of the lines
(Illustration by the author, 11 February 2015).

Pic. 4.2.9.   66
Mappings of the desiring machines produced
(Illustrations by the author, 28 November 2014).

Acknowledgments

I AM GREATLY indebted to Professor Mirka Koro-Ljungberg for her continuous support in working within post(structuralist) methodology and also for discussing the concepts of fluidity and movement with me in this book.

My HEARTFELT THANKS go to Professor Gaile S. Canella for supporting me through this writing process.

I AM DEEPLY indebted to the Laestadian women, who participated in my doctoral study, for their generous contributions.

I THANK MY daughter Amanda Rantala for her artwork on the cover of the book.

Introduction

EXAMINING CHALLENGING ISSUES within critical social inquiry sometimes requires a novel and experimental approach. It can also require the use of fluid methodologies to examine the shifting processes, the movement, the intensities and affects within the inquiry. The movement in methodology welcomes change and uncertainty by allowing the data production process, with its intensities and fluctuations, to take the lead in the inquiry. This compels the methods, the ways of inquiry, to adjust to the processes of data production and acknowledge change as an inevitable and generative disruption and opening within the inquiry. Through the disruptions, the inquiry is made explicit and the data to be seen as lived and sensed—in other words, to matter. This means that the data and the inquiry are not separate from life's processes but part of its evolution and affirmative, sustainable ethics. In this feminist poststructuralist approach, fluidity signifies open-endedness, uncertainty, and creativeness, but also responsiveness to the data, methods, methodological designs, and the ethics of inquiry. Fluidity in methodology challenges the boundaries of research by setting the inquiry in a process of constant change which makes any theory, method, or approach impossible to follow as such.

The main purpose of this book is to introduce a feminist poststructuralist approach to critical social inquiry and to demonstrate how this methodology functions in examining fluid constellations such as desire, gender, faith, and identity. The book understands inquiry as a process, and it acknowledges the multiplicity of changing elements that are part of any inquiry, its data productions, concepts, and analyses. Understanding inquiry as a process that moves in different directions than those initially anticipated makes it emergent. In this respect the flexibility and processuality of this feminist approach relates to emergent research design practices and perspectives that have been used for decades within various research paradigms and theories, but especially in feminist methodology and ethnography (e.g., Pillow & Mayo, 2014; Ramazanoglu & Holland, 2002; see also, e.g., Behar, 1993; Visweswaran, 1997). Ethnography is a practical example of emergent methodology because its ongoing data production and analysis continuously shifts the understanding of how to pursue the inquiry further (see Denzin & Lincoln, 2008).

This emergent design entails a notion that research can never be fully or completely emergent, since reassessment of how to conduct the research is based on what has been learned from prior data and analysis. This stands in contrast to a linear set of well-defined stages; therefore, an emergent design approach is often summarized as a circular process in which new data are continually being analyzed as they are being produced (see Ramazanoglu & Holland, 2002).

The emergent design approach enables flexibility in the process of inquiry in the sense that the research procedures and questions can be adjusted in response to the changing data and their analysis. It also encourages researchers to go beyond this flexibility toward fluidity of the whole research process. Fluid and emergent approaches do not limit themselves to the reflective circular movement in order to follow the route of reassessment; instead, they proceed by taking cues from the process of inquiry as a whole, while extending the definition of data to include intensities, affects, and materialities of the events and encounters in which the data are produced that go beyond the humanist subject as a center of inquiry (see Koro-Ljungberg, 2016; Koro-Ljungberg & MacLure, 2013).

These fluid methodologies similarly follow the spontaneous flow of the inquiry and allow the events and encounters to direct them, unlike the conventional research practices of collecting, transcribing, and interpreting data. Instead, fluid methodologies work toward living with the data while playing with scientific, philosophical, and literary works and ideas, which involves creating concepts and language to align with the emergent nature of the inquiry. This means creating more descriptive language to express the non-articulated events, materialities, and affects in the inquiry but also to disrupt familiar modes of thinking, writing, and doing research in favor of allowing changes, novel ideas, and orientations to emerge. This also means undertaking experiments in which the data as well as the theory and methods are understood as ongoing creations of inquiry rather than being formations applied to the inquiry. This experimental way of inquiry is part of what Henri Bergson (1911) called "creative evolution," or life as a creative movement, within which the data and their analysis are considered emergent and mobile parts of a creative unfolding beyond repetition, a search for validity, or following a method.

To explain and illuminate this fluid feminist poststructuralist approach, I introduce the methodology I used in my doctoral study and detail the productions and examination of data I produced, together with 13 women, over a three-and-a-half-year period between 2012 and 2016. The women belong to a conservative religious movement in Finland. The fluid and experimental methodologies allowed for adjustment to the shifting and unanticipated conditions of inquiry in which the focus changed from examining individual desires to exploring movements, intensities, and affects in the data. This methodological move required adopting a creative attitude toward inquiry: theories and methods served the needs of the inquiry in order to approach difference without victimization. To analyze processual data for its movement, and to produce analysis beyond judgment, required building an understanding of change and difference beyond normative, predicted ethics of inquiry.

As a feminist poststructuralist exploration, this book welcomes disturbances and irruptions as possibilities. In this sense, it is not restricted by the norms of conventional research. It is this fluid approach that attempts to further broaden the understanding of research in ways that go beyond the design and practice and toward more expansive forms of transformation in the ethics of qualitative research. Allowing for open-ended systems of inquiry, methods that are already emergent themselves—as, for instance, memory work and collaborative writing—enables an increased understanding of alternative transformative ethics of inquiry and the possibilities these carry. This does not suggest a disregarding of other ethical perspectives on research as such, but a striving for a better ethical understanding of the situatedness of research and the effects the methodologies have on the data and participants. It is also crucial to devote increased attention to questions such as: What are the outcomes of research and knowledge produced? For whom and by whose ethics was it produced? Finally, what are the political effects of the research on individuals and groups within society?

These are also the core questions in critical social research that aims to promote change and difference and question the structural inequalities in society. However, from the perspective of critical social research, poststructuralist methodologies in their fluidity can sometimes seem to jeopardize the struggle for equality as they strive to question the core of humanist ethics by opposing the idea of a stable human(ist) subject and the possibility of an objective, single truth. Nevertheless, accepting the inescapable change and the existence of a multitude of truths and a diversity of ethical perspectives makes it possible to understand the importance of approaching questions often overlooked or neglected within qualitative research due to their complexity and elusive nature.

This alternative approach, nevertheless, demands an ethical unfolding of inquiry at its processual level through events and encounters of movements, affects, and intensities in order to understand that knowledge is invented in these temporarily situated processes (Manning, 2007). In an affirmative ethics of inquiry, the normative humanist ethics are replaced by sustainable ethics in striving for social justice, as they involve residing within the movement of inquiry and engaging with its situated ethics to become aware of the inequalities and troubles the methodology undertakes to address (see Stengers, 2010/2011; Haraway, 2016). This responsibility compels fluid critical social researchers to oppose the oppressive forms of power by avoiding fixed and authoritative ideas of method, comparison, and judgment, and instead challenge the dominant ways of inquiry with more inclusive ethics that add to the possibilities of acknowledging difference as inevitable in these times of political polarization.

This book consists of three sections, each of which approaches fluid feminist poststructuralist methodologies differently. The first section introduces the approach of the book and explains the use of fluidity and methodologies in motion within qualitative inquiry. The second section demonstrates the processes of data production, analysis composition, and data analysis within fluid inquiry through a case study. The final section comprises a critical discussion of the ethical consequences and the future possibilities of the fluid feminist methodologies within critical social qualitative inquiry.

References

Behar, R. (1993). *Translated woman.* Boston: Beacon.
Bergson, H. (1911). *Creative evolution* (A. Mitchell, Trans.). New York: Henry Holt. Retrieved from https://www.gutenberg.org/files/26163/26163-h/26163-h.htm
Denzin, N.K., & Lincoln, Y.S. (2008). *Collecting and interpreting qualitative materials.* Thousand Oaks, CA: Sage.
Haraway, D.J. (2016). *Staying with the trouble. Making kin in the Chthulucene.* Durham, NC, and London: Duke University Press.
Koro-Ljungberg, M. (2016). *Reconceptualizing qualitative research: Methodologies without methodology.* Thousand Oaks, CA: Sage.
Koro-Ljungberg, M., & MacLure, M. (2013). Provocations, re-un-visions, death, and other possibilities of "data." *Cultural Studies <=> Critical Methodologies, 13*(4), 219–222.
Manning, E. (2007). *Politics of touch: Sense, movement, sovereignty.* Minneapolis and London: University of Minnesota Press.
Pillow, W.S., & Mayo, C. (2014). Feminist ethnography: Histories, challenges, and possibilities. In S.N. Hesse-Biber (Ed,), *Handbook of feminist research: Theory and praxis* (pp. 187–205). Thousand Oaks, CA: Sage. Retrieved from http://dx.doi.org/10.4135/9781483384740
Ramazanoglu, C., & Holland, J. (2002). *Feminist methodology: Challenges and choices.* London: Sage.
Stengers, I. (2010/2011). *Cosmopolitics I and Cosmopolitics II* (R. Bononno, Trans.). Minneapolis: University of Minnesota Press.
Visweswaran, K. (1997). Histories of feminist ethnography. *Annual Review of Anthropology, 26,* 591–621. Retrieved from https://www.jstor.org/stable/2952536

SECTION ONE:
FLUID CRITICAL
QUALITATIVE METHODOLOGIES

CHAPTER ONE

Motion and Fluidity in Feminist Critical Social Inquiry

> *Like the dance practice, the philosophical exploration is a technicity in its own right, activated and activating across registers of content and processual invention, moving incessantly between the rigor of denotion and the force of expression. Each of our events seeks collectively to find modalities of experimentation that connect practices at the levels of their intensive creative force. This is done not in order to map them onto one another, or to evaluate one in terms of another, but to propose a co-causal thirdness of exploration that can be generative of new modes of practice and inquiry.* (Manning & Massumi, 2014, p. 94)

EXAMINING HUMAN EXPERIENCE in today's personally and individually centered world requires rethinking and re-envisioning research methodology. Zygmunt Bauman (2000) suggests that "'fluidity' or 'liquidity' would be used as fitting metaphors when we wish to grasp the nature of the present, in many ways *novel*, phase in the history of modernity" (p. 2). Fluidity could therefore be understood as its own paradigm, which would provide novel use of methods, theories, and concepts. It is part of the postmodern movement in methodology, better known as the postmethodology which aims at temporal, flexible, and open-ended engagement with embodied subjects and communities, various knowledge production processes, and systems of belief, but also engagement with nature and environment at different levels (Koro-Ljungberg, 2012). Erin Manning and Brian Massumi (2014) turn to performativity as a transitional mechanism, which assists in creating "modalities of transition that captured not the content of the last exercise (be it artistic or philosophical) but its affective intensity (its generative force). [The language used for this] had to be language that was not simply descriptive or denotative, but conveyed a performative force" (p. 98). The challenge therefore is to make the affective intensity of experience, encounter, or event to be felt through wording and writing. This requires movement in methodology that "enables a continuous, complexifying, cross-referencing of variations," and thinking of positions as the emergent product of movement, releasing the thought of divisions to emphasize processes (Massumi, 2002, p. 156; Bergson, 1910/2010). In other words, affects and intensities are only possible to be studied and understood through methodological practices that remain in motion.

This fluidifying Bergsonian methodology stresses the essentiality of focusing on processes in critical social inquiry, and on change, affects, and intensities, while the right and wrong ways of inquiry are not the issue any longer, but the focus is on how to define an ethics of inquiry when the ground upon which they operate is constantly moving. Ability to envision the social and cultural determinations as derived and secondary to motion is required as the social is understood as unsolidified, open-ended, and relational, in which the interactions-in-the-making take different forms. The fluidifying methodology is also concerned about the difference between possibilities and potentials, as there is no grounding instance that emerges as possible, but potentials are immanent processes that become possible when formed. The challenge is to not get too hooked into the codings and positionings of cultural classifications which halt movement and label the nature of the process, since the qualitative growth of the world with its every move and change *is* the becoming cultural of nature (Massumi, 2002). This has demanded the shift toward an affirmative methodology, as Massumi (2002) writes, "techniques which embrace their own inventiveness and are not afraid to own up to the fact they add (if so meagrely) to reality" (pp. 12–13). Methodologies, which shift the paradigm toward affirmative ethics, allow the inquiry to be a creative process, but also one with effects and responsibility to the politics of now and future.

Using fluid methodologies in examining the politics of difference and marginal perspectives situates them in the field of critical social qualitative research. Traditionally, critical research examines the systems of inequity, domination, and oppression; thus, its political emphasis suggests that it focuses on the sources of the problems rather than their processes and solutions. Usually critical inquiry is seen as "openly ideological" with "a clear thread of argumentation running through the research problem, the purpose, theoretical lens, methodology, analysis, interpretations, and conclusions," but it also "has the potential to inform both policy and practice and, at the same time, to empower both researcher and participants alike" (Shields, 2012, pp. 2–3). Also, Canella and Lincoln (2012) state with Ellsworth (1989) that critical theory can be conceptualized as being "embedded within patriarchal forms of reason, ..., such that the attempted adoption of a critical lens can easily create the illusion of justice while actually reinscribing old forms of power" (p. 104).

The problem with the traditional methodologies and practices is that they do not often succeed in challenging the existing dominant and oppressive power constructions, and according to Canella and Lincoln (2012), "to illuminate the hidden structures of power, and the disempowerment of others (e.g. groups, knowledges, ways of being, perspectives)" (p. 105). This criticism urges a different brand of critical inquiry by shifting the focus from representing injustices to studying the affective processes in which inequity and oppression are voiced. The requirement of being openly ideological lays responsibility on the researcher to identify one's own perspectives on the world and to clearly state them as a basis for the inquiry. Working within fluid methodologies, the emphasis also shifts from the special care the researcher takes to conduct the research, to concern for the whole inquiry as a process with its political effects: How is the data produced and analyzed, by whom and for whom, and with what aims and consequences?

The focus on production and processes in methodology also suggests that critical inquiry does not have to limit its focus to examining the "origins," history of oppression, or on the discourses of power even if it is essentially situated and contextual. Critical inquiry should also be fluid and flexible as it deals with the constantly changing social world, the phenomena and politics of life examination, and while it requires political situatedness and contextuality of inquiry. The contextuality does not hold the inquiry in place, but changes along with the movement of methodology and the issues at hand. Also, qualitative inquiry that is fundamentally critical can be at the same time experimental and open-ended, as these do not exclude each other. Examining the movement, affects, and intensities, and acknowledging the event, the momentary setting, and milieu in its changing elements become compulsory for a valid feminist inquiry, since its coordinates need to be mapped, even momentarily, to be able to situate the knowledge produced.

To imagine a critical social qualitative inquiry that would be radically fundamental, original, and exciting (St. Pierre, 2011), but still fluid in its situatedness, requires probing larger narratives of contemporary social injustices and thinking critical social inquiry as a democratic project away from following more dominant (politically correct) orientations of academic research (Denzin & Lincoln, 2005). Denzin and Giardina (2016) suggest that we should look beyond the established methodologies, post-positivist research, and its domination to be able to understand the act of research as inherently political. Denzin and Giardina (2016, pp. 6–7) also state that this is possible through turning to "anti-foundational approaches," "methodologies without methodology," which as "marginalized" manage to challenge dominant conventions but also contribute to the need of more experimental and creative social, political, and ethical approaches to today's injustices and knowledge productions. This implies thinking beyond ready-methods and theories which proved to be impossible anyhow since ideas like concepts are not transferable in their situatedness from one event to another as methods and theory change when put together with other ideas (see further Deleuze & Guattari, 1994). Therefore, we are faced with the challenge of constantly creating concepts, methods, analyses, and novel ontological orientations to serve the needs of the inquiries at hand and the ethical, societal, or political tasks that this postmodern moment of complexity and liquidity (fluid racial, sex, and gender identities and untraceable internet, global, and local politics) requires. Additionally, to be able to imagine the future of feminist critical social inquiry as ethical we need to find more affirmative and sustainable ethics when addressing these escaping contemporary social issues (Braidotti, 2013).

In this book, creating methods and analyses is part of fluid methodologies, but also part of an ethics of feminist, poststructuralist, and critical social inquiry since the ontological orientations of the research shift with the needs of the inquiry. For instance, in a collective inquiry when the data are produced together within face-to-face encounters, the encounters dictate the movement of the inquiry. Because the encounters are constantly in flux, the methodology of inquiry needs to be continuously crafted to follow the events and their mattering intensities (see Denzin & Giardina, 2016).

1.1. Movement in methodology

The movement in methodology gives room for conceptual and theoretical inclusion and enables us to pay special attention to differences within and complexities without compelling them into categories and binaries of comparison and judgment. Conceptualizing and creating methodology in flux is to overcome the need to fix meanings and understandings, and encourages the undertaking of alternative approaches to research processes. Methodological flexibility offers "comfortableness and familiarity with epistemological and methodological diversity, and puzzlement associated with unorthodox conceptualizations of research" (Koro-Ljungberg, 2012, p. 82).

This eventhood of methodology assists in attempts to capture the affective and embodied processes of human and other encounters occurring within research processes. Therefore, understanding research through its eventhood calls for its reconceptualization within the materiality of the practices, narrative creations, and situational ethics that are involved in the inquiry. This is to muse with various relational, epistemological, and methodological ideas and events within research. Some of those ideas might resonate, co-create, and interfere with the research, affecting the inquiry and its orientation (see Koro-Ljungberg, 2012; Schostak and Schostak, 2008). Musing in its open-endedness creates both possibilities and challenges to reconceptualize and differently examine complex social questions of oppression and exclusion, which might compel ways of recognizing the colonized, misrepresented, or silenced knowledges as well as the use of diverse and otherwise non-normative lines of inquiry. This means accepting the fluctuating research process as the tenet for inquiry and not seeking external validity in, for instance, surprising results (see Massumi, 2002).

When methods, theories, research practice, and analysis are in flux they assist critical scholars to provoke social change and promote social justice, as researchers are compelled to consider what they produce with their methods, theory, and analysis of social life, and conditions under inquiry. They have to consider how their intentions meet the requirements of ethical and social justice research and how their studies can not only be further translated into actions, but also how these open-ended, flexible, and spontaneous research designs can be adjusted to work for the benefit of the researched (see Cheek, 2010). These adjustments and openness are essential while studying minority groups and seeking access to their processes, which requires accepting a particular truth and knowledge (Koro-Ljungberg, 2012). Without the flexibility of research and the openness it necessitates, it is impossible to get to examine the subtle processes going on during research, since fluid methodologies resonate with unplanned and spontaneous interventions, tacit knowledges, counternarratives, and unconventional research practices, which are all essential to promoting critical science and its changing contexts, evolving theory, and creative processes of theory formation and problem solving (Yanchar, Gantt, & Clay, 2005).

Movement in methodology enables explorations; experiments move away from researcher-led research and acknowledge the situatedness, and therefore compromised and limited nature of research productions such as data, theories, and methods, as they are already collectively co-produced descriptions and representations. The epistemological desires of the researcher tend to follow the physical locations of participants, co-currently affecting histories, stories and narrative lines, and various sociopolitical conditions, discourses, theoretical ideas, and methodological paradigms. According to Koro-Ljungberg (2012), no qualitative inquiry can be identical, nor is it possible to reconstruct again because methodological processes and their conditions are constantly in flux. Instead, methodological processes include events and interactions that would be impossible to anticipate or document. Consequently, various theoretical and methodological perspectives need to be adjusted to the requirements of the sociopolitical phenomena under examination. Methodology shapes with its ideas, ontologies, theoretical perspectives, and epistemologies the knowing that becomes possible in the inquiry. Similarly, methodology shapes how various understandings, conceptions, and policies are met and encountered. For instance, when the binary of researcher and participant roles is shaken, knowing is not a product of the methods and theories used but an escalating and unanticipated force shaping the movement within methodology.

Therefore, in critical qualitative research, knowing should not be taken for granted as an established means of power. Instead, it should be understood as a process, which is always uncertain and often unlinear in the examination of changing human and social conditions. In this process of knowing, the particular subjective immediacy of the event is given the status of the universal in thought, which makes the dualism of subject/object redundant, as the subjective immediacy is understood to be folded in the objects and entities of all kinds in the universe (Whitehead, 1978/1985). Thus, perceiving knowing as a changing and indefinite but situated process ties methodology to a different understanding of time. Time is no longer static, chronological, or singular but is understood through differenciation as multiplying and complex in its rhythm and movement (Massumi, 2002; Deleuze, 1994; cf. Lefebvre, 1992/2004). The concept of "differenciation" is understood here according to Gilles Deleuze's (1988, pp. 96–98; 1994, pp. 208–214) differential ontology separate from the concept of differentiation. As a question of variation differenciation enables us thinking seemingly unified systems like identity and gender as processes which are open to the changes time as a dynamic movement brings to these. Through differenciation, also methodology is in flux, time is no more understood through its common linear logic since time multiplies, and its multiplying affects the movement. In other words, processes, perceptions, and relations overlap, interweave, and become interrupted and inseparable. In this way the fluidity of methodologies prevents separating the process of inquiry from its durational, spatial, affective, and intuitive conditions.

Besides, the idea that methods and theories could be implemented becomes impossible as the fluidity of the methodological processes prevents the use of established methods and analysis, as movement follows intensities, tying together the situated flows of the studied phenomena and its processes, events, and interactions. So, the resulting possibility is to let the process of inquiry create a methodology at hand that fits the studied subject itself. The challenges faced with ready-made methods and attempts to implement them and their combinations (such as mixed methods, for instance) are no longer relevant since they too are constantly changing as they are affected by interactions, events, and other research designs and methodologies. Rather, the focus is now on the techniques in-the-making and ways of inquiry that emerge from the needs of the situated research and analysis.

Movement in methodology is a process which cannot be copied or reproduced, neither can it be made into a method since it has no origin to be traced. It changes within the surrounding conditions. The processual nature of this methodology enables the examination of situated perspectives connected to complex sociopolitical questions of inequality and injustice, since it is open to adjust itself to the complexities and instabilities of everyday life. This is how methodology changes within the examined conditions and each and every inquiry produces its own movement, its own processes, approaches, and interactions. Therefore, validity or the effect of inquiry cannot be measured externally only through its outcome. There is also always an element of wonder and surprise included in all research processes as the inquiry constantly changes and its outcomes and effects are yet to be seen. This changes the purpose of research from reflecting reality to producing reality as the emphasis shifts from singular knowledge to generating compound knowledges and truths in research (see Koro-Ljungberg, 2012). The movement of methodology is in the actual encounters and events in which the researchers creatively engage throughout the research process.

1.2. Fluidity

Fluidity expresses motion in an inquiry. As Zygmunt Bauman (2000) notes, "Fluids ... neither fix space nor bind time"; the concept of fluidity enables the understanding of inquiry as a simultaneously temporal and spatial process (p. 2). For Koro-Ljungberg (2016) fluidity in methodology refers to methodological spaces "where multiple things and methods occur simultaneously and where frameworks and methodological foci are diverse and continuously changing" (p. 79). In these fluid spaces, methods, tools, and approaches exist alongside but also at different times and in different forms:

> "Methods" and "tools" are not methods and tools in their stable meaning or rigid structures, but "methods and tools" begin and end in an unforeseen and unpredictable "order," forming incomplete methodologies without absolute identities or nonidentities. Methods and tools are conceptualized as temporary structures that are being regenerated again and again. Following this line of thought, methodological flows, tools, approaches, and techniques do not collapse, fail, or disappoint. Instead, they melt, transform, circumvent, infiltrate, appear, and disappear while opening up new directions for qualitative research. (pp. 79–80)

Still, this temporality of the ongoing processes makes inquiry flexible in its situatedness as it necessarily goes through the particular spacetimes, and the passing time brings continuous change (see Haraway, 1988; Bergson, 1910/2010; Deleuze, 1988; Massumi, 2002). The knowledge that the inquiry produces is therefore always in-the-making, yet still situated since the fluidity of inquiry does not prevent the knowledge from being perceived as truthful or valid, but actually makes these structured and conformist ways of thinking about knowledge redundant, and instead, stresses the significance of understanding the knowledge formation processes themselves. This perspective enables researchers to accept the uncertainty, fragmentation, and temporality that follows the use of epistemologically and methodologically novel approaches. Similarly, this involves accepting knowledge as plural, multiple, and at the same time universal and singular so that all knowledges are situated as well as constantly collectively created. Therefore, there cannot be ready-methods as the unquantifiable life events, encounters, and relations request to be studied as living entanglements and extending the object of research.

Fluidity is a way of inquiry that enables the (co)production of data to be followed, and bears well with the uncleanliness, nonlinearity, unpredictability, and onto-episte-methodological inconsistency that are often thought the opposite of valid and correct qualitative research, yet still allows the researcher to make situated analyses while following the process. Even though these encounters are in flux, they consist of specific situated knowledge about the events and the challenges they propose, which therefore need to be made as transparent as possible to make them accessible for other researchers' later extensions. For this transparency, we need to depict the events in detail to make understood the way the choices, plans, and designs were made. These open-ended elements of fluid inquiry escape linear logic and necessarily make the inquiry more challenging. Nevertheless, for the researcher the unpredicted elements and the changes in the research process often lead to deeper engagement with the inquiry as the data responds to the researcher's actions and creates understanding of the researcher's own contribution in the process of the inquiry. So, through the inquiry, from the beginning to the end, we deliberately attempt to focus and narrow down the choices we encounter, which is the only fact that separates the processes of inquiry from the processes of life.

In feminist poststructuralist theory, instead of using the term *fluidity*, its feminine counterpart, *mucosity*, can be used as a way to oppose the binary male conception that fluidity as a term entails. As feminist philosopher Luce Irigaray (1984/1993) describes,

> mucous is closer to fluidity than to solidity, yet it comes between the two like the viscous. It can expand and contract, but not necessarily in terms of shape or in a quantifiable manner. It has no solid permanence and no given form, yet it constitutes the primal material tissue or membrane upon which solidity and permanence ground their form. (as cited in Martin 2000, p. 156).

As viscous in its simultaneous consistency and movement, mucosity actively adapts to the given circumstances, symbolizing and embracing difference and the idea of the other. Despite mucous being placed within female body, within the lips and the uterus, and beyond masculine abstract and dichotomous conceptions, it is still not reduced into a passive tissue; rather, it is an active movement which is never still but comes and goes in the half-open (Martin, 2000). Thus, mucosity seems to add to the understanding of fluidity as a never seizing movement even though it could be seen as a politically opposite force to masculine fluidity. Since mucosity has an inbuilt tendency to include and understand otherness as complex but complementing multiplicity, it could be perceived as an intensification of the more common concept of fluidity as it also includes the core of feminist methodology: subtleness, inclusiveness, and openness to differences—elements that each and every critical social inquiry should involve to encounter the injustices and complexities of life. Furthermore, in its viscerality mucosity makes for a useful concept in studying difference as a lived experience as it brings in another level of understanding toward difference beyond binary thinking. Although mucosity as a term manages to include complexities of life and situational ethics in studying social phenomena and difference yet it is not as versatile in depicting movement and change within research as a whole (as fluidity is). On the contrary, the concept of fluidity adapts well in addressing and describing the movement and the processuality of inquiry and enables the changes in the processes to be examined.

1.3. "Subjects" of situated knowledges

In feminist poststructuralist thought the subject is understood as the outcome of a variety of collective and social productions such as expressions, articulations, and discourses but also beyond the nature/culture binary as ecological production (see Colebrook, 2000). Similarly, feminist poststructuralist theory attempts to examine subjects outside the dichotomic order of opposites such as mind/body, theory/practice, and singular (individual)/collective, decentering interest from the normative Western white male subject and its individualistic human ethics in social inquiry (Colebrook, 2000; Conley, 2000; Flieger, 2000; see Braidotti, 2003, 2008). Also, the ethico-aesthetics theory proposed by Félix Guattari (1995, 1997, 2013) manages to shift the theorizing of the mind-body relationship beyond the subject-object divisional thinking as it seeks to depict the processes of subjectivity formation through visible and traceable mappings (see also O'Sullivan, 2010; cf. Foucault, 2005).

These poststructuralist theories, equally to the feminist postcolonial theories, approach subjectivity through its alterings and processual elements, but the latter also manages to analyze the impact of racialized gender constructions on subjectivity. The difference that fluid methodologies make on the analysis of subjectivity, or analysis of any social construction for that matter, is that they view the categories of identity as shifting, within which claiming acceptable memberships becomes unnecessary but also impossible (see Kelly, 1997). Within these methodologies, the subject is considered fundamentally *different* but not different from but different within the variation that occurs in any identification process (Bignall & Patton, 2010). Rosi Braidotti (2011) explicates this further by writing that,

> Western thought has always functioned through dualistic oppositions that create subcategories of otherness or "difference-from." Because, in this history, difference has been predicated on relations of domination and exclusion, to be different-from came to mean to be [worth] "less than." (p. 138)

The postconial understanding of a subject is therefore needed to be able to accept that the category of "subject" is not unchanging, universal, or free while existing within a "transhistorical state of othered oppression" (Chambers & Watkins, 2012, p. 298). As Mohanty (1984) states, "Western feminist discourse and political practice is neither singular nor homogeneous in its goals, interests or analyses" (p. 334); therefore, the term "feminism" as itself cannot be treated as a stable, transhistorical, critical, and political position.

In poststructuralist thinking, the subject's knowledge does not emerge as a unity outside oneself nor does oneself exist as a unit separate from the world. As much as the knowledgeable subject is part of the world, the world is part of one's subjectivity, as Deleuze states with Foucault:

> Seeing means knowing (savoir), but we do not see what we speak [of], nor do we speak [of] what we see ... Everything is knowledge, and this is the first reason why there is "no savage experience": there is nothing beneath or prior to knowledge (Deleuze, 2006, p. 90)

For Deleuze, it is part of the intra-active discursive and non-discursive, living and non-living processes that keep making the subject: It is important to be able to perceive knowledge as situated in order to be able to understand difference as crucial for collective production (Deleuze, 2006, pp. 89–90). Hence, understanding knowledge as situated is not a question of relativism; rather, it is a shift of focus in thinking from individually possessed knowledge to the various shared and continuous processes of knowledges. Likewise, postmodern research provides powerful tools for individuals to reconceptualize their everyday existence in the world, but equally it promotes diverse and minor ways of knowing (Lather, 1991; Spivak, 1999). It addresses the need to engage with decentered ways of knowing and obliges us to make sense of experience through exploring the conditions within which it emerges, as Haraway's (1988) important reminder defines the feminist vision and perception of the world: "Feminist objectivity means quite simply situated knowledges" (p. 581). With this she criticizes the claimed objectivity of traditional science (see also Deleuze, 2006), which, in her opinion, has emphasized the human and its subjectification while it has neglected the significance of the other-than-human/non-human processes.

In understanding the social, psyche, and nature to be intertwined and in flux, Guattari (1989, 1995) claims that we cannot talk about subjects, but processual components of subjectification since this positioning would impede the inevitable change in the processual constellations without leaving room for complexity and differenciation, the inevitable multiplying processes of life. Yet again, the notion of fluidity assists in comprehending the self as a process of which movement can be traced through modalities like actions, expressions, and enunciations (Manning, 2013). Like Guattari, Manning (2007) understands expressions as never singular, but always as becoming a relation within spacetime:

> An emphasis on expression leads us away from signifying a subject to becoming a relation. Expression is not reserved for the single voice of the speaking subject: expression dialogically produces chronotopes that expand the intervals between speakers and listeners. These intervals are not voids between discrete bodies; they are space-times alive with intonations, invocations, perturbations. (p. 111)

Moving beyond subjectivity to its modalities, comprising intensified clusterings of articulations and manifestations, enables difference to be understood as essential for change as the breaks, cuts, and variations for movement. When the focus is on complexity and change, the movement in methodology stands for multiple truths and ethics and against inequality, oppression, and exclusion based on difference.

Even though poststructuralist methodology has managed to deconstruct clichés as the autobiographical *I* as the individual agent and as the mediator in the creation of texts as well as the personal accounts as truthful reflections of one's life (e.g., Denzin, 1989/2014; Davies et al., 2001), the discursive constitution of the subject that relies on the instability of its documentations and interpretations often produces the subject as fragmented. Open methods and fluid ways of inquiry assist in going beyond the deconstructed individual subject, bringing out the embodied and affective nature of negotiations and processes from the otherwise discursive and symbolic productions while it challenges constructions of difference and normativity (see, e.g., Lather, 2007, 2016; Barad, 2003, 2007).

Working with feminist poststructuralist methods and the issue of differences requires accepting that there is no "past" to recall, but the simultaneous existence of past and present. The fluidity of the past marks difference as the split moment, a break or an intervention into this flux, which enables the actualization of the past in experience (see Braidotti, 2005/2006). These experiences emerge through disconnection from their first appearances due to processes of differenciation. These are the processes of internal splitting, difference-in-itself taking place in subjects and objects (see Deleuze, 1994). This is helpful in describing difference as separate from the universal term used to overcome, equalize, or neutralize gender, racial, or other differences; instead, it is the internal dynamic of open-endedness generating ever-more variation (Grosz, 2005). Difference is therefore not the opposite of sameness (see Minh-ha, 1988; Barad, 2014; Deleuze, 1994), but it enfolds it, as the past is not recurring but occurs simultaneously with the present and the future.

References

Barad, K. (2003). Posthumanist performativity: Toward an understanding of how matter comes to matter. *Signs: Journal of Women in Culture and Society, 28*(3), 801–831.

Barad, K. (2007). *Meeting the universe halfway: Quantum physics and the entanglement of matter and meaning.* Durham, NC: Duke University Press.

Barad, K. (2014). Diffracting diffractions: Cutting together-apart. *Parallax, 20*(3), 168–187.

Bauman, Z. (2000). *Liquid modernity.* Cambridge: Polity Press.

Bergson, H. (1910/2010). *Matter and memory.* (N.M. Paul and W. S. Palmer, Trans). Digireads.com Publishing.

Bignall, S., & Patton, P. (2010). Introduction. Deleuze and the Postcolonial: Conversations, negotiations, mediations. In S. Bignall & P. Patton (Eds.), *Deleuze and the postcolonial* (pp. 1–19). Deleuze Connections. Edinburgh: Edinburgh University Press.

Braidotti, R. (2003). Becoming woman: Or sexual difference revisited. *Theory, Culture & Society, 20*(3), 43–64.

Braidotti, R. (2005/2006). Affirming the affirmative: On nomadic affectivity. *Rhizomes. Cultural Studies in Emerging Knowledge.* Issue 11/12. Retrieved from http://www.rhizomes.net/issue11/braidotti.html

Braidotti, R. (2008). In spite of the times: The postsecular turn in feminism. *Theory, Culture & Society, 25*(6), 1–24.

Braidotti, R. (2011). *Nomadic subjects: Embodiment and sexual difference in contemporary feminist theory.* New York: Columbia University Press.

Braidotti, R. (2013). *Posthuman.* Cambridge: Polity Press.

Canella, G.S., & Lincoln, Y.S. (2012). Deploying qualitative methods for critical social purposes. In S.R. Steinberg & G.S. Canella (Eds.), *Critical qualitative research reader* (pp. 104–114). New York: Peter Lang.

Chambers, C., & Watkins, S. (2012). Postcolonial feminism? *The Journal of Commonwealth Literature, 47*(3), 297–301.

Cheek, J. (2010). Human rights, social justice, and qualitative research: Questions and hesitations about what we say about what we do. In N.K. Denzin & M. Giardina (Eds.), *Qualitative inquiry and human rights* (pp. 100–111). Walnut Creek, CA: Left Coast Press.

Colebrook, C. (2000). Introduction. In I. Buchanan & C. Colebrook (Eds.), *Deleuze and feminist theory* (pp. 1–17). Edinburgh: University Press.

Conley, V.A. (2000). Becoming-woman now. In I. Buchanan & C. Colebrook (Eds.), *Deleuze and feminist theory* (pp. 18–37). Edinburgh: University Press.

Davies, B., Dormer, S., Gannon, S., Laws, C., Rocco, S., Lenz Taguchi, H., & McCann, H. (2001). Becoming schoolgirls: The ambivalent project of subjectification. *Gender and Education, 13*(2), 167–182.

Deleuze, G. (1988). *Bergsonism*. (H. Tomlinson & B. Habberjam, Trans.). New York: Zone Books.

Deleuze, G. (1994). *Difference and repetition* (P. Patton, Trans.). New York: Columbia University Press.

Deleuze, G. (2006). *Foucault* (S. Hand, Trans. and Ed). London: Continuum.

Deleuze, G., & Guattari, F. (1994). *What is philosophy?* (H. Tomlinson & G. Burchell, Trans.). New York: Columbia University Press.

Denzin, N. K. (1989/2014). Interpretive biography. *Qualitative research methods, 17*. London: Sage.

Denzin, N.K., & Giardina, M.D. (2016). Introduction. In M.D. Giardina & N.K. Denzin (Eds.), *Qualitative inquiry through a critical lens* (pp. 1–16). New York: Routledge.

Denzin, N.K., and Lincoln, Y.S. (2005). Introduction: The discipline and practice of qualitative research. In N.K. Denzin & Y.S. Lincoln (Eds.), *The Sage Handbook of Qualitative Inquiry* (3rd ed., pp. 1–32). Thousand Oaks, CA: Sage.

Ellsworth, E. (1989). Why doesn't this feel empowering? Working through the repressive myths of critical pedagogy. *Harvard Educational Review, 59*(3), 297–324.

Flieger, J.A. (2000). Becoming-woman: Deleuze, Schreber and molecular identification. In I. Buchanan and C. Colebrook (Eds.), *Deleuze and feminist theory* (pp. 38–63). Edinburgh: University Press.

Foucault, M. (2005). *The Hermeneutics of the subject: Lectures at the Collège de France 1981–1982*. (G. Burchell, Trans.). New York: Palgrave MacMillan.

Grosz. E. (2005). Bergson, Deleuze and the becoming of unbecoming. *Parallax, 11*(2), 4–13. http://doi.org/ 10.1080/13534640500058434

Guattari, F. (1989). The three ecologies. (C. Turner, Trans.). *New formations*, (8), 131–147.

Guattari, F (1995). *Chaosmosis. An ethico-aesthetic paradigm*. Bloomington & Indianapolis: Indiana University Press.

Guattari, F (1997). Du transfert au paradigme esthétique: Conversation avec Bracha Lichtenberg-Ettinger/ From transference to the aesthetic paradigm: Interview with Bracha Lichtenberg-Ettinger. *Canadian Review of Comparative Literature*, 611–621.

Guattari, F (2013). *Schizoanalytic cartographies*. (A. Coffey, Trans.). London: Bloomsbury.

Haraway, D.J. (1988). Situated knowledges: The science question in feminism and the privilege of partial perspective. *Feminist Studies, 14*, 575–599.

Irigaray, L. (1984/1993). *An ethics of sexual difference*. (C. Burke & G.C. Gill, Trans.) Ithaca, NY: Cornell University Press.

Kelly, U. (1997). *Schooling desire: Literacy, cultural politics, and pedagogy*. New York: Routledge.

Koro-Ljungberg, M. (2012). Methodology is movement is methodology. In S.R. Steinberg & G.S. Canella (Eds.), *Critical qualitative research reader* (pp. 82–90). New York: Peter Lang.

Koro-Ljungberg, M. (2016). *Reconceptualizing qualitative research. Methodologies without methodology*. Thousand Oaks, CA: Sage.

Lather, P. (1991). *Getting smart. Feminist research and pedagogy within the postmodern*. London: Routledge.

Lather, P. (2007). *Getting lost: Feminist efforts toward a double(d) science*. Albany: State University of New York Press.

Lather, P. (2016). Killing the mother? Butler after Barad in feminist (post)qualitative research. In A.B. Reinertsen (Ed.), *Becoming earth: A posthuman turn in educational discourse collapsing nature/culture divides* (pp. 21–30). Rotterdam: Sense Publishing.

Lefebvre, H. (1992/2004). *Rhythmanalysis: Space, time and everyday life*. London: Continuum.

Manning, E. (2007). *Politics of touch. Sense, movement, sovereignty*. Minneapolis and London: University of Minnesota Press.

Manning, E. (2013). *Always more than one*. Durham, NC: Duke University Press.

Manning, E., & Massumi, B. (2014). *Thought in the act. Passages in the ecology of experience*. Minneapolis & London: University of Minnesota Press.

Martin, A. (2000). *Luce Irigaray and the question of the divine*. London: Maney Publishing.

Massumi, B. (2002). *Parables for the virtual*. Durham, NC: Duke University Press.

Minh-ha, T. T. (1988). Not you/like you: Post-colonial women and the interlocking question of identity and difference. *Inscriptions*, Special issue *Feminism and the Critique of Colonial Discourse*, 3–4. Retrieved from https://culturalstudies.ucsc.edu/inscriptions/volume-34/trinh-t-minh-ha/

Mohanty, C.T. (1984). Under Western eyes: Feminist scholarship and colonial discourses. *Boundary 2*, *12*(3), 333–358. Retrieved from http://www2.kobe-u.ac.jp/~alexroni/IPD%202015%20readings/IPD%202015_5/under-western-eyes.pdf

O'Sullivan, S. (2010). Guattari's aesthetic paradigm: From the folding of the finite/infinite relation to schizoanalytic metamodelisation. *Deleuze Studies*, *4*(2), 256–286.

Schostak, J., and Schostak, J. (2008). *Radical research: Designing, developing and writing research to make a difference*. London: Routledge.

Shields, C.M. (2012). Critical advocacy research: An approach whose time has come. In S.R. Steinberg & G.S. Canella (Eds.), *Critical qualitative research reader* (pp. 2–13). New York: Peter Lang.

Spivak, G. (1999). *A critique of postcolonial reason. Toward a history of vanishing present*. Cambridge, MA: Harvard University Press.

St. Pierre, E.A. (2011). Postqualitative research: The critique and the coming after. In N.K. Denzin & Y.S. Lincoln (Eds.), *The Sage handbook of qualitative research* (4th ed., pp. 611–626). Thousand Oaks, CA: Sage.

Whitehead, A.N. (1978/1985). *Process and reality* (Corrected ed,). D.R. Griffin & D.W. Sherburne (Eds.). New York: The Free Press.

Yanchar, S., Gantt, E. and Clay, S. (2005). On the nature of a critical methodology. *Theory & Psychology*, *15*(1), 27–55.

CHAPTER TWO

Feminist Poststructuralist Methodologies as Escape

FEMINIST POSTSTRUCTURALIST METHODOLOGIES offer various critical perspectives for viewing the world that are often oriented toward shared data productions, experimental processes, and analyses. These methodologies assist in exploring the politics of being, with the focus on minority knowledges and how to approach them ethically. Also, feminist researchers have long pointed out the interwoven relationship between ontology, epistemology, the bias, and the absence of value neutrality in science. Equally, they have challenged established truths and critically examined the processes of human experience in which the truths are constantly made, as there exists no normative or certain absolute knowledge or truth to measure against. Still, these pioneering and situated approaches are often neglected as non-valid in the normative scientific world for their immeasurable messiness and leakiness, and therefore their value is often recognized only through a struggle (Ramazanoglu & Holland, 2002; see also Rosser, 2008).

However, this situatedness of feminist inquiry makes it ideal for examining marginalized subjects as it gives room for unorthodox ways of inquiry, opposes foundationalism, and questions the existence of absolute knowledge and single truth, while favoring approaches to inquiry which are constantly under formation, fluid, and open-ended (see Harding, 1991; Lather, 1997; St. Pierre & Pillow, 2000). This infinite and fluid nature of inquiry also requires changing the focus from subjects to processes of inquiry. Therefore, instead of aiming to trace actual voices, the aim is at following the events, intensities, and affects in the inquiry (Deleuze, 1995; Lorraine, 2000). As these open-ended infinite processes constantly evolve and change, there are no ready methods to return to as they are always in the making and cannot be captured and repeated.

This open-endedness assists in accepting the complexities and multiplicities involved in the process of inquiry, while embracing non-judgmental ethics based on the idea that there exist no unbiased and independent positions from which to observe the world, since all the ideas and perspectives are at least temporarily situated (Deleuze, 1998; Lather, 1997, 2007). Within feminist inquiry experimenting is one possible way to "enter" processes that otherwise seem impossible to examine because of their fluidity and escaping nature, and while it works toward methodologically transparent research it brings the research process and its challenges in for discussion (see, e.g., Renold & Ringrose, 2011; Ringrose & Coleman, 2013; Ringrose, 2011, 2015). The validity of experimental inquiry is in the particularity of the situation studied, with its people, place, time, and affects, as well as in the transparent process of the production of data and analysis. Therefore, experimental methodology builds understanding of the process of the inquiry, as it examines the inquiry in its situatedness and temporality. By bringing surprise and wonder to the process of inquiry it manages to question the expectations of linearity and predictability of scholarly research while enabling the understanding of change as essential for nurturing sustainable ways of being and knowing (see Deleuze, 1995).

2.1. What is feminist poststructuralism?

Poststructuralism "offers critiques and methods for examining the functions and effects of any structure or grid of regularity that we put into place," according to St. Pierre and Pillow (2000, p. 6). It is skeptical toward metanarratives (Lyotard, 1984), but it claims that cultural narratives and discourses are social constructions, and therefore, their processes of production are worth examining. Poststructuralism deconstructs the prevailing structures and reveals ways in which dominant discourses keep us "performing" within "conventional meanings and modes of being" (Davies, 1990, p. 1). It enables us to see ways in which cultural narratives are produced, regulated, and productive of the subject.

Poststructuralist theory questions what is assumed to be normal or common sense (Weedon, 2004), and therefore helping to make visible the normative forces (Davies, 2000), since it is a "mode of analysis [that] shifts attention from individualism to subjectivity, from text to discursive practices, and from signifier to signifying practices" (Kelly, 1997, p. 19). The necessary move is from meanings to processes, in which events and encounters become data, as practice always enfolds acted performed thinking, making the thinking and acting coincide so that the one is not possible without the other (see Manning & Massumi, 2014, p. vii). In poststructuralism, the attempt is to gain understanding of what it is to be a human, a subject, and to question the legitimacy of these understandings, while bringing previously marginalized experiences to the fore and to be examined.

Poststructuralist perspectives reject understanding language as communication (Sarup, 1993). Instead, they endorse alternative theories of language in which words do not axiomatically mirror the world as words do not carry meanings in or of themselves but are always part of particular cultural narratives (Deleuze & Guattari, 1994). This situatedness of language makes it productive in shaping our understandings of the world (Weedon, 2004), but similarly, as significant effort is invested into producing the discursive and interactive every day processes of life, the produced and arbitrary nature of language dissolves the difference between fiction and lived experience, making everyday a fictive reality as well as lived, experienced, and articulated (see Gough, 1991; Davies, 2000).

A feminist stance brings a political agenda to poststructuralist theory (Lather, 1997, 2001; McKenzie, 2005) as it works to expose power relations and oppressions associated with gender, race, class, able-bodiedness, and sexual orientation. Similar to poststructuralist theory, feminist poststructuralism contests the ideas of individual knowledge and objective truth as such and therefore takes a particular interest in language and how we communicate our experiences, and how that shapes the way we see the world (Flax, 1990). This feminist approach to inquiry troubles the traditional ways of inquiry through their creative and novel notions of data and processes of analysis (Britzman, 1995; Gough & Whitehouse, 2003; Kumashiro, 2004; Weedon, 2004).

Feminist poststructuralist research necessarily calls for a linking of knowledge-making practices to theoretical perspectives and theories to real-life encounters to promote critical explorations of the knowledge that we produce, its effects, and the ways that we produce it. Using a feminist poststructuralist lens enables us to become critical of the historical truths and understandings, and allows us to see into the social, political, historical, and economic influences that construct the discriminative structures in society. It allows different ways of knowing, through the body as a site of ethics and knowledge that questions the researcher as the knower. By troubling the limits of knowledge, feminist poststructuralist research sets knowledge and its production as the problem of inquiry, aiming for a "less comfortable social science," one that is undeniably political, but able to examine its own ethics and production of knowledges while being ready to be surprised by the future (Lather, 2000, p. 285). As feminist methodology focuses on the ontological, epistemological, and ethical questions, it is an important tool in identifying subjugating forces and how they operate and constitute inequalities and affect the way we word the world.

2.2. Feminist writing practices

Despite the in-built idea of the Western male human subject and his role as an author of his life (Denzin, 1989/2014), autobiography has been employed among feminist theorists to decenter the act of writing from its historical context to serve the purposes of empowering marginal and subjugated women (see, e.g., de Beauvoir, 1958; Rich, 1976). This has produced a specific female way of writing that aims to escape the victimizing effects of categorical thinking to generate knowledge within situated embodied practices. This writing offers a space in which the non-normative storylines and alternative cartographies replace the common and normative constructions of identity and accounts of life (e.g., Cixous, 2013; Irigaray, 1984/1993; Kristeva, 1980; Moi, 1985/1990; see also Ettinger, 2006).

Feminist writing, and especially feminist autobiographical writing, is closely connected to the process of identity formation, as autobiography enables one to constitute a temporary account of one's life (Butler, 2010). Besides the feminist philosophers, like Cixous, Kristeva, Irigaray, and Moi, there is a long history of feminist writers using writing as an emancipatory practice (e.g., Chopin, 1899/1981; Woolf, 1927/1994; Lorde, 1983). Writing offers access to identity formation processes as both singular and collective, and in this way, the authors can re-create their pasts as collective acts of self-justification rather than as self-documentation (see Denzin, 1989/2014). Emphasizing the social effects of the writing instead of highlighting its therapeutic value or empowering potential has made women's writings often more political than biographical.

To be able to resist discourses that subjugate requires an awearness of the restrictions of language, while moving toward more processual and affective ways of expression to contest the binaries of theory and practice (see, e.g., Woolf, 1931/2015). Close to this is the idea of "Écriture feminine" with which Hélène Cixous (2013) has ordered women to free themselves from using the male-centered language and challenge the oppressive effects of the patriarchal control of rhetoric with the feminist rhetorical tradition. Cixous (1993) advises women to focus on themselves as authors and their own embodied histories in writing narratives, creating spaces for female authorship and embodied expression. She teaches women in their writing to evoke rather than define and to use symbols and metaphors, but also to forget the linear timespaces to reject the established patriarchal order. For her, the practice of self-expression concentrates on articulating the new ways of being and knowing through exploring the borderlines/dangerous places (see e.g., Tamboukou, 2010; van der Tuin, 2014).

This practice of self-expression is elaborated further in Bronwyn Davies's work in which she produces knowledge differently through writing:

> The inclusion of my embodied self in this body of writing is not in order to produce an autobiographical account of a particular life, but because the detail of the texts of life as I have lived it as an embodied being provide an immediate and vivid resource for examining the constitutive power of discourse both as I find myself constituted and as I, in turn, constitute the world in my reading and writing of it. It is examining one's own subjective take-up of the tangled threads of life. (2000, pp. 10–11)

Davies exemplifies here how to follow one's senses and intuition, and listen to the narratives of one's body, but to avoid considering these embodied texts as individual constructions, since these texts are to be perceived as affectively lived but collectively made (Davies & Gannon, 2006, 2012). Thus, in this sense feminist poststructuralist inquiry is both singular and collective (see Nancy, 2000), since it escapes the essentialist expectations of seeking to find individual agency or voice in the written texts (Davies, 2000; Mazzei, 2010, 2016; St. Pierre & Pillow, 2000). In this practice, voice is considered to be a part of the humanist and individualist construction of an agentic subject, which marginalizes all other than the Western white male subject. Within these ethics, voice is given to the marginalized others, who are perceived as victimized and in need of agency, voice, and emancipation. To avoid this positioning, feminist poststructuralist inquiry stresses the simultaneous movement of different elements in the production of writing, by which it cannot be limited solely to either the individual or the collective.

Having access to someone else's narrative changes the limits of one's own subjectivity. This does not mean, however, that one can easily enter and understand others' experiences, but getting familiar with the conditions in which these experiences were constituted may open new paths in one's thinking. Within this it becomes possible to consider our enunciations and articulations as "figurations... a living map, a transformative account of the self that... outlines our own situated perspective," as Rosi Braidotti (2002, pp. 2–3) explicates. These figurations allow us to identify as subjects through the changing events by mapping the coordinates of our processes (see Butler, 1990, 1992). In other words, as these narrative processes are always situated by current events and conditions there is no expectation of personal narratives and experience, but rather depictions of the processes in which they are articulated.

2.3. Memory work and collective biography

> You don't write with your ego, your memory, and your illnesses. In the act of writing there's an attempt to make life something more than personal, to free life from what imprisons it. (Deleuze, 1995, p. 143)

Memory work was originally a group method that involved collective analysis of individually written memories. Frigga Haug with her collaborators (1997) developed the method to combine theory and experience to explore the processes whereby women become agents in society. With its emancipatory aim, they examined the women's everyday practices by deconstructing and reconstructing these experiences. For Haug (1987) memory work had the benefit of enabling the researcher to use the past as data for reflection since the aim was to highlight the subjectively significant events and recollections as well as their reconstructions to be seen as the inevitable elements in the formation of the self (see, e.g., Crawford, Kippax, Onyx, Gault, & Benton, 1992; Onyx & Small, 2001). Within this thought, Haug (1987) defended the significance of subjective experience against critiques that concerned its validity and generalizability. However, her perspective impeded the understanding of experience as collectively produced, since it positioned experience in the subject and in its reflected individual memories, which fixed the thinking to the subject-object binary and therefore worked against the aim of the practice to produce memories collectively. To overcome this binary Bronwyn Davies and Susanne Gannon (2012) developed Haug's memory-work practice into "collective biography" that moved in a Deleuzian sense from affection and perception to affect and to percept, toward understanding memory as a collectively produced event that is not entirely subjective nor shared in its nature (p. 357).

Working on one's memory could be understood as an act that immediately places the subject in the past (Bergson, 1911/1991; Deleuze, 1988a; Grosz, 1999). This past constructs memories as separate durational entities fused together in encounter-production (Deleuze, 1994, 1988a), which means that memories are perceived as virtual (re)collected affective visions (see Ansell Pearson, 2001), and remnants of the perception that is left after other interests are taken away (see Deleuze, 1988a). Affect is also enfolded in the memory and composed within its various processes such as expressions, articulations, images, and experiences (Bergson, 1910/2010; Deleuze, 1988a; see also Massumi, 2008, 2015). Within a Spinozian understanding, affect is as an ability to affect and to be affected (Deleuze, 1988b), as it takes different forms from atmospheres, feelings, and reactions to embodied and produced intensities and sensations as the affect exceeds individual and bounded human bodies and existence (Blackman, 2015). Since affect materializes and represents itself within everyday life it assists in capturing the simultaneous factual and figurative aspects of human productions (see Dolphijn & van der Tuin, 2012).

The movement and interplay of the two processes, the recollections and their productions, constitute memory as instantaneous rather than enduring, which is then capable of tying these movements together as new recollective arrangements (Deleuze, 1988a). Therefore, in attempting to capture memories, they slip and get lost within the shifting events. Memory does not reside in the folds of individual brains; rather, memory is the enfoldings of space-time-matter written into the universe, or better, on the enfolded articulations of the universe in its mattering, as Karen Barad (2007) describes:

> Memory is not a record of a fixed past that can ever be fully or simply erased, written over, or recovered (that is, taken away or taken back into one's possession, as if it were a thing that can be owned). And memory is not a replay of a string of moments, but an

> enlivening and reconfiguring of past and future that is larger than any individual. Re-membering and re-cognizing do not take care of, or satisfy, or in any other way reduce one's restraints; rather, like all intra-actions, they extend the entanglements of which one is part. The past is never finished. It cannot be wrapped up like a package or a scrapbook . . . we never leave it and it never leaves us behind. (p. x)

Memories actualize in the break between repetitions, in other words, a memory is produced by a break in the connective flow. Repetition does not produce a copy of the memory of the past, nor does it function to replace the things that have not been heard, perceived, or understood. It is not the constructed anticipation of future moments either. On the contrary, because the past cannot be repeated, repetition is therefore always a new production, because the immanent past or future is not there to be reflected upon. Deleuze (1994) describes this as reminiscence:

> Reminiscence confuses the being of the past with a past being, and since it is unable to assign an empirical moment at which this past was present, it invokes an original or mythical present. The importance of the concept of reminiscence . . . consists in its manner of introducing time or the duration of time into thought as such. (p. 142)

The present is a discontinuous movement whose rhythm we attempt to follow. However, the movement of the present is impossible to capture or to embrace, since the rhythm breaks when it is described and the intensity of it is lost. This is explicit, for instance, in the way our awareness of a situation affects it as it slows down our actions while also making us more attentive. The changing present makes it impossible to reflect upon and reproduce. It is not only because the past does not exist and cannot be traced, but because the present brings new connections causing the past to change. This differenciation is found in the midst of events escaping the present in which memories and future exist only in order to be created again, as the past is just the point of departure for new beginnings.

2.4. COLLABORATIVE DATA PRODUCTION

The feminist poststructuralist writing offers a break from the strictures of the traditional, phallocentric, and authoritarian approaches by emphasizing subtle, sensitive, and entangled intra-actions between the writers and their productions (Davies & Gannon, 2006, 2012). Writing collaboratively is to share the process of writing without necessarily seeking to produce a shared text or multiple authorships, but rather, sharing the experience of producing text together. Writing collaboratively is therefore not preordained (Richardson & St. Pierre, 2018), as it always works toward different purposes depending on the event and the encounter. Collaborative writing often works as a subtle inquiry, but instead of orientating toward subtleness and shared experience, it can operate to surprise, interfere, and experiment. Hence, it extends the understanding of collaborative work to include uneven and unexpected elements while challenging the idea of predictable, comfortable, and collectively produced writing (Koro-Ljungberg & Ulmer, 2016), and while showing how open the collaborative work of writing is to different approaches and uses.

Wyatt, Gale, Gannon, and Davies (2011) suggest that writing works within experience, which is understood as a creation formulated through the intersective concepts, percepts, and affects that fold and refold together in the given moment. Therefore, Wyatt et al. (2011, p. 2) call collaborative writing "immanent planes of compositions" in which the writers aim to remain as close as possible to the event of writing while concurrently sharing their affects of it with others. As it is not an individual composition of elements, the text evolves, connects, changes, and sometimes also ceases to flow, enabling one to live the events of someone else's articulated experience as your own beyond the timely synchronized act of writing. In following the moments that the encounters have to offer these instant compositions shift the understanding of memories toward perceiving them as both collective and personal as well as unintentional and inclusive productions. This production of data is neither clearly a method, but it is about engagement in encounters and narratives, and the processes these include. It is also about open sets of time: the past as well as the now, not as accountable but as exciting movement in between (see Ansell Pearson, 2001). In collective writing, the past is the present as the event of writing itself is always already about the past in the present.

From this point of view, fluidity in data production is about engaging in the moment and its potential and being open for the unexpected (Massumi, 2002; see also Rantala, 2017), since this unexpectedness gives space to wonder but requires being "attentive and open to surprise" (MacLure, 2013, p. 231). Deleuze (2004) also suggests that "To the extent that events are actualized within us, they wait for us and invite us in" (p. 169). One way to do this is to follow the movement of the inquiry, to be ready to experiment and to be surprised, and to take nothing for granted, not even the smallest flicks of the contributions these moments have on offer.

References

Ansell Pearson, K. (2001). Pure reserve: Deleuze, philosophy and immanence. In M. Bryden (Ed.), *Deleuze and religion* (pp. 141–155). London: Routledge.

Barad, K. (2007). *Meeting the universe halfway: Quantum physics and the entanglement of matter and meaning*. Durham, NC: Duke University Press.

Bergson, H. (1910/2010). *Matter and memory*. (N.M. Paul and W. S. Palmer, Trans.). Digireads.com Publishing.

Bergson, H. (1911/1991). *Time and free will*. Edinburgh: Neill and Co. Ltd.

Blackman, L. (2015). Researching affect and embodied hauntologies: Exploring analytics of experimentation. In B.T. Knudsen & C. Stage (Eds.), *Affective methodologies* (pp. 25–44). London: Palgrave Macmillan.

Braidotti, R. (2002). *Metamorphoses: Towards a materialist theory of becoming*. Cambridge: Polity Press.

Britzman, D. (1995). Is there a queer pedagogy? Or stop reading straight. *Educational Theory, 45*(2), 151–165.

Butler, J. (1990). *Gender trouble*. London: Routledge.

Butler, J. (1992). Contingent foundations: Feminism and the question of postmodernism. In J. Butler & J. Scott (Eds.), *Feminists theorize the political* (pp. 3–21). London: Routledge.

Chopin, K. (1899/1981). *The awakening*. New York: Bantam Classic.

Cixous, H. (1993). *Three steps on the ladder of writing*. New York: Columbia University Press.

Cixous, H. (2013). *Meduusan nauru ja muita ironisia kirjoituksia* [The Laugh of the Medusa]. (H. Rundgren & A. Sevón, Trans.). Helsinki: Tutkijaliitto.

Crawford, J., Kippax, S., Onyx, J., Gault, U., & Benton, P. (1992). *Emotion and gender: Constructing meaning from memory*. London: Sage.

Davies, B. (1990). The problem of desire. *Social Problems, 37*(4), 501–516.

Davies, B. (2000). *A body of writing, 1990–1999*. Walnut Creek, CA: Alta Mira Press.

Davies, B., & Gannon, S. (2006). *Doing collective biography*. Maidenhead, Berkshire, England: Open University Press.
Davies, B., & Gannon, S. (2012). Collective biography and the entangled enlivening of being. *International Review of Qualitative Research, 5*(4), 357–376.
de Beauvoir, S. (1958). *Mémoires d'une jeune fille rangée* [Memoirs of the dutiful daughter]. Èditions. Paris: Gallimard.
Deleuze, G. (1988a). *Bergsonism*. (H. Tomlinson & B. Habberjam, Trans.). New York: Zone Books.
Deleuze, G. (1988b). *Spinoza: Practical philosophy*. (R. Hurley, Trans.). San Francisco: City Lights Books.
Deleuze, G. (1994). *Difference and repetition*. (P. Patton, Trans.). New York: Columbia University Press.
Deleuze, G. (1995). *Negotiations 1972–1990*. (M. Joughin, Trans.). New York: Columbia University Press.
Deleuze, G. (1998). *Essays critical and clinical*. (D.W. Smith & M.A. Greco, Trans.). Burchill, London: Verso.
Deleuze, G., & Guattari, F. (1994). *What is philosophy?* (H. Tomlinson & G. Burchell, Trans.). New York: Columbia University Press.
Denzin, N.K. (1989/2014). Interpretive biography. *Qualitative research methods, 17*. London: Sage.
Dolphijn, R., & van der Tuin, I. (2012). *New materialism: Interviews & cartographies*. Open Humanities Press. Retrieved from http://hdl.handle.net/2027/spo.11515701.0001.001
Ettinger, B.L. (2006). Matrixial trans-subjectivity. *Theory, Culture & Society, 23*(2–3), 218–22.
Flax, J. (1990). *Thinking fragments. Psychoanalysis, feminism, and postmodernism in the contemporary West*. Berkeley: University of California Press.
Gough, A., & Whitehouse, H. (2003). The "nature" of environmental education research from a feminist poststructuralist viewpoint. *Canadian Journal of Environmental Education, 8*, 31–43.
Gough, N. (1991). Narrative and nature: Unsustainable fictions in environmental education. *Australian Journal of Environmental Education, 7*, 31–42.
Grosz, E. (1999). Becoming... An introduction. In E. Grosz (Ed.), *Explorations in time, memory and futures* (pp. 1–12). Ithaca, NY, and London: Cornell University Press.
Harding, S. (1991). *Whose science? Whose knowledge? Thinking from women's lives*. Ithaca, New York: Cornell University Press.
Haug, F. (1987). *Female sexualisation. A collective work of memory*. London: Verso.
Irigaray, L. (1984/1993). *An ethics of sexual difference*, (C. Burke & G.C. Gill, Trans.). Ithaca, NY: Cornell University Press.
Kelly, U. (1997). *Schooling desire: Literacy, cultural politics, and pedagogy*. New York: Routledge.

Koro-Ljungberg, M., & Ulmer, J. (2016). This is not a collaborative writing. In M.D. Giardina & N.K. Denzin (Eds.), *Qualitative inquiry through a critical lens* (pp. 99–115). New York: Routledge.

Kristeva, J. (1980). *Desire in language. A semiotic approach to literature and art.* (T. Gora, A. Jardine & L. S. Roudiez, Trans.). New York: Columbia University Press.

Kumashiro, K. (2004). *Against common sense: Teaching and learning toward social justice.* New York: Routledge.

Lather, P. (1997). Drawing the line at Angels: Working the ruins of feminist ethnography. *Qualitative Studies in Education, 10*(3), 285–304.

Lather, P. (2000). Drawing the line at Angels: Working the ruins of feminist ethnography. In E.A. St. Pierre & W.S. Pillow (Eds.), *Working the ruins: Feminist poststructural theory and methods in education* (pp. 284–311). New York: Routledge.

Lather, P. (2001). Postbook: Working the ruins of feminist ethnography. *Signs: Journal of Women in Culture and Society, 27*(1), 199–227.

Lather, P. (2007). *Getting lost: Feminist efforts towards a double(d) science.* Albany: State University of New York Press.

Lorde, A. (1983). *Zami: A new spelling of my name.* Trumansburg, NY: The Crossing Press.

Lorraine, T. (2000). Becoming-imperceptible as a mode of self-presentation: A feminist model drawn from a Deleuzian line of flight. In D. Olkowski (Ed.), *Resistance, flight, creation. Feminist enactments of French philosophy* (pp. 179–194). Ithaca, NY, and London: Cornell University Press.

Lyotard, J. F. (1984). *The postmodern condition.* Minneapolis: University of Minnesota Press.

MacLure, M. (2013). The wonder of data. *Cultural Studies <=> Critical Methodologies, 13*(4), 228–232.

Manning, E., & Massumi, B. (2014). *Thought in the act. Passages in the ecology of experience.* Minneapolis & London: University of Minnesota Press.

Massumi, B. (2002). *Parables for the virtual.* Durham, NC: Duke University Press.

Massumi, B. (2008). Of microperception and micropolitics. An Interview with Brian Massumi. *INFLeXions No. 3—Micropolitics: Exploring ethico-aesthetics.* Retrieved from http://www.inflexions.org/n3_massumihtml.html

Mazzei, L. (2010). Desiring silence: Gender, race and pedagogy in education. *British Educational Research Journal,* iFirst Article, 1–13.

Mazzei, L. (2016). Voice without a subject. *Cultural Studies <=> Critical Methodologies, 16*(2), 1–11.

McKenzie, M. (2005). The "post-post period" and environmental education research. *Environmental Education Research, 11*(4), 401–412.

Moi, T. (1985/1990). *Sukupuoli/Teksti/Valta. Feministinen kirjallisuusteoria.* [Sexual/Textual Politics: Feminist literary theory] (R. Koli, Trans.). Tampere: Vastapaino.

Nancy, J.L. (2000). *Being singular plural.* Stanford, CA: Stanford University Press.

Onyx, J., & Small, J. (2001). Memory-work: The method. *Qualitative Inquiry, 7*(6), 773–786.

Ramazanoglu, C., & Holland, J. (2002). *Feminist methodology. Challenges and choices.* London: Sage.
Rantala, T. (2017). Maternal mo(ve)ments in memory work. A special issue of *Reconceptualizing Educational Research Methodology.* https://doi.org/10.7577/rerm.2554
Renold, E., & Ringrose, J. (2011). Schizoid subjectivities? Re-theorizing teen girls' sexual cultures in an era of 'sexualization'. *The Australian Sociological Association, 47*(4), 389–409.
Rich, A. (1976). *Of woman born: Motherhood as experience and institution.* New York: W.W. Norton & Company.
Richardson, L., & St. Pierre, E.A. (2018). Writing. A method of inquiry. In N.K. Denzin & Y.S. Lincoln (Eds.), *Handbook of qualitative research* (5th ed., pp. 818–838). Thousand Oaks, CA: Sage.
Ringrose, J. (2011). Beyond discourse? Using Deleuze and Guattari's schizoanalysis to explore affective assemblages, heterosexually striated space, and lines of flight online and at school. *Educational Philosophy & Theory, 43*(6), 598–618.
Ringrose, J. (2015). Schizo-feminist educational research cartographies. *Deleuze Studies, 9*(3), 393–409.
Ringrose, J., & Coleman, R. (2013). Looking and desiring machines: A feminist Deleuzian mapping of bodies and affects. In J. Ringrose & R. Coleman (Eds.), *Deleuze and research methodologies* (pp. 125–144). Edinburgh: University Press.
Rosser, S. (2008). Gender inclusion, contextual values, and strong objectivity. In S. Nagy Hesse-Biber & P. Leavy (Eds.), *Handbook of emergent methods* (pp. 53–72). New York: Guilford Press.
Sarup, M. (1993). *An introductory guide to post-structuralism and postmodernism* (2nd ed). Athens: University of Georgia Press.
St. Pierre, E.A., & Pillow, W.S. (2000). Introduction. In E.A. St. Pierre & W.S. Pillow (Eds.), *Working the ruins. Feminist poststructural theory and methods in education* (pp. 1–24). New York: Routledge.
Tamboukou, M. (2010). Charting cartographies of resistance: Lines of flight in women artists' narratives. *Gender and education, 22*(6), 679–696.
van der Tuin, I. (2014). Diffraction as methodology for feminist onto-epistemology: On encountering Chantal Chawaf and posthuman interpellation. *Parallax, 20*(3), 231–244.
Weedon, C. (2004). *Feminist practice and poststructural theory* (2nd ed). Malden, MA: Blackwell Publishing.
Woolf, V. (1927/1994). *To the lighthouse.* Ware, Hertfordsire: Wordsworth Editions Limited.
Woolf, V. (1931/2015). *The waves.* New York: Oxford University Press.
Wyatt, J., Gale, K., Gannon, S., & Davies, B. (2011). *Deleuze and collaborative writing: An immanent plane of composition.* New York: Peter Lang.

SECTION TWO:
FLUID METHODOLOGIES
IN SPECIFIC CONTEXTS

The purpose of this section is to introduce one possible way of working with fluid methodologies through a study, its data production, and analysis. The section has three chapters, which each present parts of the study: its context and data production, the composition of analysis and the actual data analysis. Chapter three unfolds the context of the study, the process of data production, and discusses the use of feminist poststructuralist methodology. Chapter four opens up the composition of the data analysis process, and chapter five depicts the data analysis through selected excerpts, and it also gives a short summary of the analysis.

CHAPTER THREE

Overview of the Method

TO WORK IN special context that could be sensitive requires care in how one approaches the research. Feminist ethnographic studies often stress the researcher's power to decide on the foundations, concepts, and aims of the research. Especially in examining personal and sensitive matters, the researcher is compelled to give account and unfold the premises and locations from which the inquiring is done to be able to consider the ethical matters otherwise easily neglected in the research process (see Lappalainen, Lahelma, Hynninen, Kankkunen, & Tolonen, 2007; Oinas, 2001; Rantala & Kuusisto, 2013). Since feminist inquiry is often explicitly political in its aim for social change, its ontological, epistemological, and methodological premises are at the center of the interest. In practice this means open discussions about the presuppositions, theoretical ideas, and methods of the inquiry to make explicit the situatedness of the researcher and her/his knowledge: what is known, from where and how (see Haraway, 1988).

3.1. A BRIEF CONTEXTUALIZATION OF THE STUDY

The women in the study belonged to the Conservative Laestadian movement, which is part of the Evangelical Lutheran Church of Finland. Laestadianism has roots in German pietism, which is known for its rigid confessionalism and hardening of Lutheran doctrine (Brown, 1978; Stoeffler, 1973). The Laestadian movement was founded on the work of a Swedish-Sami botanist and a preacher, Lars Levi Laestadius (1800–1861). Laestadius's teachings gained popularity among the Swedish-Sami revivalists in Karesuando in Swedish Lapland in the 19th century (Nykänen, 2012), as he preached for moral awakening through a strong personal belief and continuous repentance of sins (Joensuu, 2016; Laestadius, 1906/1970, 1968; Pyysiäinen, 2004). The next century great schisms and expansions separated Laestadianism into small independent congregations (see, e.g., Talonen, 2001), and since then it has evolved into an extensive "educational Christianity" while maintaining a close communal lifestyle (Suolinna & Sinikara, 1986, p. 156). There are an estimated 200,000 Laestadians worldwide, most of whom live in Finland, in Northern Ostrobothnia, but also in Sweden, Norway, and North America.

Currently in Finland the Laestadian women are at the center of media discussions, since the movement's negative attitude toward the use of birth control is viewed as a human rights issue. The dispute concerning Laestadian women's reproductive rights is closely connected to the feminist debates about women's status and agency in conservative religious movements in general (see, e.g., Avishai, 2008; Mahmood, 2012; Gallagher, 2004). Motherhood has a special significance to the Laestadian movement: a young unmarried Laestadian woman changes from being a sister to being the mother of a large family. Therefore, women are referred to as mothers and sisters in Laestadinism, since womanhood and femaleness are both associated with female sexuality, which is considered a taboo. This makes maternal identity the only officially recognized identity for an adult Laestadian woman. Paradoxically, female sexuality is seen as an uncontrollable force and therefore sinful and dangerous even while it is still vital for procreation, and for continuation of the movement (Alasuutari, 1992; see also Ihonen, 2001; Kutuniva, 2007).

The current transformational politics in Conservative Laestadianism has questioned the subjugated role of women and their limited and regulated status as mothers in the movement. This transformation has an in-built feminist agenda, which embraces women's individuality, emancipation, and freedom while it also presents motherhood as embodied subjugation in the movement. The transformation has managed to endorse women's rights in the movement, and especially their right to use birth control, while nevertheless, it has also fortified the upsurge of the movement's opposite prevailing conservative ethos, which endorses the importance of motherhood and housewifery, but also the men's exclusive right to preach and therefore to lead the life in the community. This conservative "turn" seems to work as a backlash against current transformational politics; while the modern wing of the movement seems to move toward more open and inclusive politics, the conservative wing seems to move toward even more conformist ways and values, such as highlighting the separate duties for men and women in the communities.

With the help of transformational politics Laestadians have been able to question the conservative values of the movement, endorse Laestadian women's right to use contraception, and promote women's opportunities to pursue their own education and career paths more freely. It has, thus, empowered Laestadian women to fight subordination, which threatens to make them mere instruments of the movement's reproductional aims. This empowerment is also explicitly endorsed in both the current academic studies as well as literature on Laestadianism (Nissilä, 2013; Toivio, 2013; Hintsala & Kinnunen, 2013; Rauhala, 2013; Pylväinen, 2012). As the future of the Laestadian movement depends greatly on women's engagement in reproduction, women's aspirations and public expressions play a crucial role in negotiations of the movement's future. Thus, whatever the women decide to do is significant for the movement and its continuation; however, the current political transformation, perhaps unintentionally, disregards the diversity of women's aspirations. Likewise, it has failed to assess its own politics, which position the women as victimized and seems not to recognize the multiplicity and complexity of the women, and perhaps for this reason, the needed diversity is missing in the discussions on Laestadian womanhood and motherhood.

Research interests.

First, my main interest was to examine Laestadian women's aspirations concerning their identity, and especially the way media represented the women. To do that, I wanted to produce data with the women themselves to study their processes. My study therefore placed emphasis on women's aspirations, even though such aspirations constantly change in relation to social and religious norms and expectations among other processes. Therefore, in the analysis I focused on examining the women's negotiations concerning their desired subjectivities with the following research questions:

1. *What kinds of formations of subjectivity do the Laestadian women's aspirations produce?*

1.1. *How do these processes intertwine, yet also differ in connection to faith, collectivity, and womanhood?*

Though the number of participants was limited, the data produced were quite extensive both in diversity and density. The women, of various ages and from various backgrounds, communities, and regions, had differing views on the politics of the contemporary Laestadian movement. Still, most importantly, the women who participated wanted to belong to the movement and to become mothers, but at the same time they desired to claim female identity and to position themselves as women in the movement. As previously discussed, Laestadian women are often expected to identify themselves as mothers, and not as women, and so for Laestadian women to claim female identity is still seen as provocative gesture in many Laestadian communities. Therefore, the aim of the study was not simply to depict the women negotiating their identity within Laestadian religious laws and doctrine, but to examine their aspirations as intersections of, for instance, personal, social, and religious processes. Thus, in contrast to traditional social inquiry, the focus was not on bringing the past encounters and events into the present to reconstruct the women's aspirations, but to examine these aspirations as processes-in the-making.

3.2. The data production

The three-and-a-half-year inquiry took place between the autumn of 2012 and winter of 2016. During the first set of data, autobiographical writings (between September 2012 and March 2013), I became acquainted with eight women, who introduced my study in their communities or to the Laestadian women they knew. Four of the informants were successful in finding participants. The challenge was in the exclusiveness of the movement, especially now, when Laestadian women were at the center of national media interest. In the end, 13 women participated in the first part of the study, the writing assignment, and four women continued on to the follow-up study.

The writing assignment produced 13 pieces of autobiographical writing, and the follow-up study, the face-to-face encounters, produced 19 hours of recorded material. I made a logbook of the encounters and the events of the sessions to assist in finding the excerpts, but I also made transcriptions of some parts of the recordings. The third data production took place before, after, and between the face-to-face encounters and comprised pieces of writing and prose. At the time of the study, the women were between 19 and 45 years of age, and they mostly came either from the rural areas in the north, northwest of Finland or near Helsinki. Among the women were students who were still single as well as married mothers with small children. Their educational backgrounds ranged from no secondary education to a doctoral degree and their occupational status from being a student, housewife, or professional to being self-employed.

Feminist wording processes: writing against the grain.

In contrast to ethnographical research, where the researcher seeks to create a deep understanding of the studied field and its social and material circumstances through her presence (Gordon & Lahelma, 2003; Tolonen & Palmu, 2007), in a writing assignment the researcher's presence "comes in" through the instructions given. Therefore, a writing assignment does not necessarily include interaction in the traditional sense, but the instructions and questions influence the process of writing even though the everyday and embodied experience of writing guides the writing as well (Cixous, 1993; Davies, 2000; Davies et al., 2001). In the task, the aim was to grasp some of the conditions in which the women negotiate their gender and identity, and therefore, with this task I located the writers temporarily in the process of growing up into a woman. I also encouraged the women to imagine their future as women in the movement and to express their hopes for the future.

Additionally, the aim of the writing task was to "provoke" and inspire the women to write against the grain—to question the given location and frame in order to produce new ways of thinking, but also to learn to read the internal complexity and multiplicity of gendered narratives as complementary rather than contradictory (see Davies, 1993). The instructions included questions on the women's experiences of growing up in the Laestadian movement: *How would you describe your life and yourself as young? Has the way you see yourself changed, and if so, how? If you think about your family and friends, what kind of women do you see? What hopes and dreams do you have for the future?* These questions were included to help the women to begin their writing, but also to orientate them to write about their aspirations:

> **DESCRIPTIVE NARRATIVE 3.1:**
> I am not one of those who understand the elegance of rings, jewellery, perfumes, and high heels. I have joked about it that my husband has to be someone very masculine or either very feminine . . . to suit someone like me—a little manly-like woman. :) I am a woman

who wants to show that women have strength and options. Even if according to some views, we were born to give birth, we have life, feelings and will, which we are allowed and have the right to use. (Autobiographical writings data, 2012–2013)

Most of the women's texts sent for the task were autobiographical in style but they still followed loosely the given topics. The level of intimacy varied in the writings as some were lengthy accounts of life often written in a chronological order from childhood to the present, including descriptions of life changes and personal development, and on the contrary, some of the writings were clearly political in discussing societal norms concerning women and discussing the use of contraceptives, women's status, and future in the movement. Compared to the handwritten pieces, which came through mail, the pieces sent by email were more spontaneous, as they had more errors and a less organized structure:

Pic. 3.1.1.
Photo of handwritten autobiographical writings (Autobiographical writings data, 2012–2013).

> **DESCRIPTIVE NARRATIVE 3.2:**
> I realize that I connect womanhood with motherhood when thinking of my own mother. Maybe, I do not think of people especially as women and men, but more as individuals. Again, I notice that the things that have something to do with being a woman I discuss with my mother. (Autobiographical writings data, 2012–2013)

The instructions in the autobiographical writing task were there to inspire the women to write based on their momentary embodied experience (Cixous, 1993). The interest was in what the women wanted, aspired to, and dreamed about, and how would they express these aspirations in writing (see Richardson, 1994). However, the women's texts were not understood as implications of individual experiences and desires, nor were they understood as a undirectional practice or

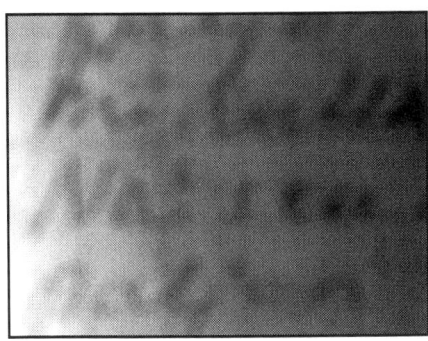

Pic. 3.1.2.
A close-up photo of a writing (Autobiographical writings data, 2012–2013).

creation that flows from author to page; rather, the texts were better explained as cartographies, mapped points, and lines of expression (Braidotti, 2002, 2003). They were mappings of enunciations, discourses, and practices, which had "nothing to do with signifying . . . [but] with surveying and mapping," as Deleuze and Guattari explain (1987, p. 5). Language as situated process has no meaning outside of its context, and it is neither translatable nor removable (Deleuze, 1995), and therefore, writing can be seen as a situated act of mapping, as it is only understood within its own context, constitution, and connections:

> **DESCRIPTIVE NARRATIVE 3.3:**
> My uncle's wife was the biggest inspiration in my life that time. Through her way of living I could see that there was another kind of womanhood, much more bold and womanlike, feminine. She wore high heels and I had seen her using tampons. Still somehow, I understood that all this was forbidden. Nevertheless, I was eagerly breathing her spirit and everything she was; all the new and exciting.
> (Autobiographical writings data, 2012–2013)

As language is often one of the outcomes of the processes under study, it needs to be examined together with its constitutive event and its movement, intensities, and affects, in which these articulations materialize and "the notional meets the motional" as we nonsensuously perceive edgings of movement become language, as the language "tweaks" into the rhythm of movement, as Manning and Massumi elaborate (2014, p. 51). The concept of event assists in verbalizing these processes by embracing momentariness, and therefore it becomes possible to study the productions that occur in the moments of the inquiry and provides understanding of past events as situatedly co-produced within space and its multiple elements (Massumi, 2002; see also Davies, 2014; Haraway, 2004).

I consider the generative nature of feminist writing a practice that has special importance for enabling the recognition of difference. For instance, in the study, the writing enabled the depiction of disputed, diverse, and complex accounts as it created data also on the specific points, events, and encounters (see Massumi, 2006). The writing practice enabled the women's enunciations and articulations to be seen as collective processes including changes, distractions, and deviations, which could not be taken as accounts of individual experience as such, but could be understood as mappings of the processes in which their aspirations were formed. As with the writing, the attempt was to explore how women's experience was entangled with other processes in order to challenge the thinking of the singular and the collective (Davies & Gannon, 2006; see Haug, 1987), instead of producing "conventionalized, narrative expressions of life experiences" (Denzin, 1989/2014, p. 7). This was to move further from practices of knowledge construction (e.g., Haug et al., 1987; Ramazanoglu & Holland, 2002; Skeggs, 1997, 2004), and toward understanding knowledge as an open-ended process entangled with embodied and multiple other mattering processes within and beyond the social (see Braidotti, 2005/2006).

A follow-up study: the spaces of tears, laughter, and silences.

The writing task proceeded into arranging face-to-face encounters to work on the affects and intensities of the writings. This process of writing, like any process that involved the past, brought the recollections and affects into the present, which was especially important as we were dealing with processes usually viewed as private and sensitive. In the letter to the women and instructions of the writing assignment, I suggested that we write about our embodied and affective memories. With this suggestion, I attempted to follow the idea of "Écriture feminine" as an inspiration to create our own way of writing and bring in the bodily felt, sensed, and affected dynamics in the writing. The feminist writing offered a challenge by requesting to include embodiedness and practicing self-expression. This was to live in the moment and to depict the bodily felt events and the processes experienced in one's writing in which our spoken and written memories could not be understood as reflections of the past, instead, these were intuitive takes on so-called memory, which led us to inhabit the events of memory and to form them again differently in the writing.

However, the women were unwilling to respond to the given ideas of writing about our embodied memories and this convinced me that the sessions could not be planned, and it both required and enabled an alternative way of working. Therefore, the next sessions with the women focused on themes that emerged spontaneously, and included stories, comments, and expressions. The writing seemed to occur in similar ways; everyone produced spur-of-the-moment texts that did not necessarily adhere to the themes discussed. This spontaneity seemed to work for us, and it enabled us to let the discussions take the lead. Nevertheless, these wandering discussions required using a quite different approach to data production than merely following a "method," as this experimentality of the collective data production assisted in acknowledging that as much as we created within the events and encounters of the study, they created us and our data.

This experimentality guided also the data production away from seeking to construct narratives and instead let the stories to come out as they effortlessly would, allowing changes, breaks, and asymmetries to flourish. Then the affective intensities in the moment sometimes led into silent moments and tears but also laughter (see, e.g., Davies, 2009; Rantala, 2018). Similarly, our correspondence altered during the data production. The longer we worked together, the more detailed and subtler the texts became. There were some challenges due to the fact that we worked on intimate and personal levels. Sometimes awkward moments and disagreements occurred, but compassion was also always present in the encounters as we attuned to one another's stories, cries, and laughter.

> **DESCRIPTIVE NARRATIVE 3.4:**
> I catch myself feeling sorrow for someone, some of the experiences are easy to share, but some I cannot "enter"... In the morning... I am late, I am in a hurry... I feel like [through the discussion] I could find an access to my own feelings... I enjoy talking so that I can see the faces, expressions of others, hear the voices, the breaks, the tones...
> (Collaborative writings data, 2013)

As we understood that there was no plan or "technique" we created our own understanding of these encounters as invitations to experiment, to follow the emerging events and encounters and practice listening carefully to others. Bronwyn Davies calls this "emergent listening," a pedagogical practice that aims to understand the situational ethics of our actions and focuses on the intensities and ethics of an event in social encounters (Davies, 2014, p. 21). This immanence of the encounters assisted in living through each others' joys and sorrows:

> **DESCRIPTIVE NARRATIVE 3.5:**
> [As I started my work,] the first three [years] were very difficult, since I was pregnant the first two ... but during the third ... I had a baby. (Collaborative writings data, 2013)

The openness of the account depicts the subtleness but also the intensity of the experience in the group. For one of our sessions, we had written stories of our lives to each other, to read and to comment on, stories that followed the form of the earlier writing assignments in their narrative style but differed greatly in their openness and detailed descriptions. The texts below are from the same author, but the first text was sent for the writing assignment and the second for the face-to-face encounters. However, these texts are not presented to compare their level of "truthfulness" based on the openness of the accounts, but to picture the different moments affecting the writing.

> **DESCRIPTIVE NARRATIVE 3.6:**
> I grew up and independent very early on and moved away from home already after secondary school ... When younger, I had a good group of friends to go out with to the meetings. We shared our joys and sorrows and enjoyed carefree time as young women. (Autobiographical writings data, 2012)
>
> The secondary school was a very difficult time for me as I was bullied for being Laestadian. I was at a very vulnerable [st]age and I constantly thought about what I was like and what others thought of me. And the fact that I was then constantly "hit in the face" has affected my self-esteem my whole life. (Collaborative writings data, 2013)

In the sessions, the philosophical and ontological questions concerning our identity and the limits of collectiveness were pondered on. Despite the usually smooth and interweaved flow of discussions and stories in our data production, there also appeared differences and misunderstandings causing ruptions to the flow. These breaks formed "opportunities" for marking something off from particular wholeness (Barad, 2007, p. 197), but by cutting into the flow they also invited further discussions (see MacLure, 2013). For us, cutting was a particular event in the production of memories which made it possible to perceive memories as collective productions, part of the feminist way of understanding our existence as relational. Within this reading we understood ourselves not as isolated subjects but as part of relational processes (see Davies & Gannon, 2012). This relationality was explicit in the encounters as it managed to blur the limits of my story and your story and me and you (Davies, 2009, p. 9):

> **DESCRIPTIVE NARRATIVE 3.7:**
> I continue thinking, what am I? How am I constituted? What is me? My thoughts, feelings, experiences. This is me, there is nothing else [of me]. The question about the boundaries between the revival movement and me, made me think . . . what is me and what is the movement??? What is the recognizable dissection, cut, between the generations? Where is it? (Collaborative writings data, 2013)

The struggles of confining the limits of us enabled the correspondence to be spontaneous, initiated by someone starting a chain of writing and then someone responding to that with their text. This processual nature of the writing enabled these collaborations to work over long distance in a kind of spur-of-the-moment space:

> **DESCRIPTIVE NARRATIVE 3.8:**
> I have not been able to write for a while, even if I wanted to. I have been sick—with tiredness and shivers—so I have taken it easy, one day at a time. Somehow, I feel that I have become very inefficient! There are days when . . . cooking the everyday meal is a challenge! (Collaborative writings data, 2014)

The way we lived through each other's wordings made these encounters much more than just a process of inquiry to us. To me, even if everyone had their (s)pace to write and read in, this was about sharing personal experiences while sensing there is someone in that co-encounter and spacetime, enlivening these experiences with compassion and understanding (see Ettinger, 2006; Davies & Gannon, 2012).

3.3. Fluidity and movement in feminist data production

In feminist poststructuralist methodology, knowledge is understood as collectively produced within the daily lives and experience of people (see Ramazanoglu & Holland, 2002; Skeggs, 2004); likewise, the collective production changes the researcher's role from being the "knower" to being a member of the data production process. For instance, in the face-to-face discussions and writing I was part of the group despite being a non-Laestadian. Therefore, my participation in the data production could have been seen as compulsory due to the ethics of feminist inquiry, according to which any inquiry always involves the people and elements present and makes it impossible for the researcher to conduct research objectively without affecting the data production or being affected by it her/himself (Haraway, 1988). However, in my case my participation was not a question of me not being willing to attend, but a question of being accepted in, the acceptance which I assume was granted due to my family background in the Laestadian movement. The women felt I was "acquainted enough with the Laestadian traditions" (Recorded data, 2013).

These previously discussed feminist methods of inquiry, such as memory work, differ in the ways they organize data production. For instance, the women in my study were not academics who had the previous experience of writing and publishing together, unlike the women in many other feminist studies (Davies et al., 2001; Davies & Gannon, 2006; Gannon, 2001; Haug et al., 1987). In collaborative work with non-academics, on one hand, there is often pressure for the researcher to take on more responsibility than the other members; on the other hand, the power the researcher has over the inquiry, such as in the decisions about analysis or outcomes of the inquiry, situates the researcher differently in the group and affects the whole idea of collaborative work and its ethics.

In our case, the collaboration meant us working together without all of us having a common academic background and therefore not sharing the understanding of the studied topic. This situation, however, enabled *co-researching*, which shifts the power structure in the group by placing the academic researcher into the inquiry also as an object and vulnerable subject of research (Haug, 1987; Crawford, Kippax, Onyx, Gault, & Benton, 1992). Even if I was both researcher and researched in the data production, I was still not able to share the authorship since we did not share the knowledge required to work together on the methodology. Also, we were not able to discuss the studied subject in scholarly terms, by using theories and philosophical concepts, which would have enabled us to analyze the data together. So, even if we produced the data and the ideas together, the research was still part of a scholarly study and left to me to complete.

Since the researcher can write and publish a collaboratively produced work independently of the other participants and therefore benefit from the research, the power in research is not equally distributed, and special ethics of inquiry need to be addressed and adopted. This involves thinking in terms of how the participants could benefit from the research process beyond the ready-set academic goals: what does the inquiry enable them to do that they would not be able to do otherwise (see Frost, Eatough, Shaw, Weille, Tzemou & Baraitser, 2012)? Feminist inquiry demands research ethics that go beyond research transparency and having the participants' consent to publish the data. Feminist ethics compels the researcher to be aware of and responsible for the outcomes and possible harms and effects the research might have on its participants and requires the researcher to be fully aware of heavy personal contributions involved; as Patti Lather (1991) rightly puts it, we researchers must understand "what it means for lives to become data" (p. 99).

Feminist research ethics also highlight subtleness in handling personal and sensitive data, and taking complex matters, such as anonymity, seriously (e.g., Liamputtong Rice, 2000; Lee, 1993; Longman, 2007; Oinas, 2001; Stanko, 1997). For instance, the Laestadian women chose anonymity, which on one hand protected them from the possible negative and harmful effects their identification could have had on their personal lives in their small communities, but which on the other hand impeded them from taking part in endorsing their position, in person, in the movement. Despite ensuring the data were handled with consideration, still the study, like any other study, could result in serving unexpected aims and purposes beyond the intentions of the researcher or the participants. This demonstrates the ethical complexity of social research, which needs to be considered when studying human lives, in which the participants share their life with a researcher who is hopefully aware of the responsibility and equally able to respond to it.

However, the ethics, as well as the understanding of ethics, may shift during a study. For instance, while planning the assignments, I assumed the issue of womanhood (gender) to be a sensitive topic for religious women to discuss, especially as the term "woman" seemed to connote sinfulness within the Laestadian official discourse. This expectation, which most probably derived from my childhood memories of Laestadian community, at first prevented me from generating an alternative approach to the data (see St. Pierre, 1997). However, womanhood proved to be a well-contemplated and readily articulated concept among the women, enabling us to discuss the affective and embodied processes they attached to it.

The women's willingness to engage in face-to-face sessions and the study's focus being on processes enabled us to proceed with an open-ended structure, with encounters and writing beyond specific ready-set aims and predictable outcomes. This open-endedness of the sessions enabled the data production to evolve, making the inquiry flexible and open to disruptions and surprises. Even though we did not know each other, and each of us had a different idea of the encounters and their purposes, as the events took the lead in the encounters, they freed us from attempting to follow any method, leaving us open to scientific adventure and to let events become the data.

This experimental and collective nature of the inquiry shifted its ethical focus from handling issues considered sensitive and non-normative, such as pious women's aspirations and identifications, to examining them as processes in-the-making beyond victimization and comparison. This focus being on the processes, which are always both singular and collective, makes them less problematic to study; as the collective is multiple, it is never a universally representable unity of singularities or representative of the total singularity (see Ansell Pearson, 2001). For this reason, using terms such as "pious women," always demands clarification to be able to identify these terms beyond categorical and subjugating positionings (Braidotti, 2003; Deleuze & Guattari, 1987). This means, for instance, that the Laestadian women were not only to be perceived through their belonging to the conservative religious movement but also through their aspirations and the processes that aspiring collectively created. This allowed viewing the women and their aspirations through their multiple, connected, changing, and differing processes, even when religiously aimed. Understanding change and processuality as an essential part of conceptualizing difference contributes also to the understanding of research ethics more broadly to concern not just the specific matters and questions under study but also the ontological, epistemological, and methodological processes of inquiry as a whole.

References

Data
Writings data, November 2012–April 2013
Recorded data from the face-to-face sessions, 19–20 April 2013 and 29 December 2013
Collaborative writing data, February 2013–January 2016

Literature
Alasuutari, P. (1992). Ehkäisyn kiellon synty ja umpikuja vanhoillislestadiolaisessa herätysliikkeessä [The origin and the deadlock of the birth control debate in Conservative Laestadianism]. *Sosiologia, 2*, 106–115.
Ansell Pearson, K. (2001). Pure reserve. Deleuze, philosophy and immanence. In M. Bryden (Ed.), *Deleuze and religion* (pp. 141–155). London: Routledge.
Avishai, O. (2008). "Doing religion" in a secular world. Women in conservative religions and the question of agency. *Gender & Society, 22*(4), 409–433.
Barad, K. (2007). *Meeting the universe halfway: Quantum physics and the entanglement of matter and meaning*. Durham, NC: Duke University Press.
Braidotti, R. (2002). *Metamorphoses: Towards a materialist theory of becoming*. Cambridge: Polity Press.
Braidotti, R. (2003). Becoming woman: Or sexual difference revisited. *Theory, Culture & Society, 20*(3), 43–64.
Braidotti, R. (2005/2006). Affirming the affirmative: On nomadic affectivity. *Rhizomes. Cultural studies in emerging knowledge*. Issue 11/12. Retrieved from http://www.rhizomes.net/issue11/braidotti.html
Brown, D. (1978). *Understanding pietism*. Grand Rapids: Eerdmans Publishing Co.
Cixous, H. (1993). *Three steps on the ladder of writing*. New York: Columbia University Press.
Crawford, J., Kippax, S., Onyx, J., Gault, U., & Benton, P. (1992). *Emotion and gender: Constructing meaning from memory*. London: Sage.
Davies, B. (1993). *Shards of glass: Children reading and writing beyond gendered identities*. Cresskill, NJ: Hampton Press.
Davies, B. (2000). *A body of writing 1990–1999*. Walnut Creek, CA: Alta Mira Press.
Davies, B. (2009). Introduction. In B. Davies & S. Gannon (Eds.), *Pedagogical encounters* (pp. 1–16). New York: Peter Lang.
Davies, B. (2014). *Listening to children. Being and becoming*. Abingdon: Routledge.

Davies, B., Dormer, S., Gannon, S., Laws, C., Rocco, S., Lenz Taguchi, H., & McCann, H. (2001). Becoming schoolgirls: The ambivalent project of subjectification. *Gender and Education, 13*(2), 167–182.

Davies, B., & Gannon, S. (2006). *Doing collective biography*. Maidenhead: Open University Press.

Davies, B., & Gannon, S. (2012). Collective biography and the entangled enlivening of being. *International Review of Qualitative Research, 5*(4), 357–376.

Deleuze, G. (1995). *Negotiations 1972–1990*. (M. Joughin, Trans.). New York: Columbia University Press.

Deleuze, G., & Guattari, F. (1987). *A thousand plateaus: Capitalism and schizophrenia*. (B. Massumi, Trans.). Minneapolis: University of Minnesota Press.

Denzin, N.K. (1989/2014). Interpretive biography. *Qualitative Research Methods, 17*. London: Sage.

Ettinger, B.L. (2006). *The matrixial borderspace. (Essays from 1994–1999)*. Minneapolis: University of Minnesota Press.

Frost, N., Eatough, V., Shaw, R., Weille, K.L., Tzemou, E., & Baraitser, L. (2012). Pleasure, pain, and procrastination: Reflections on the experience of doing memory-work research. *Qualitative Research in Psychology, 9*, 231–248.

Gallagher, S.K. (2004). Where are the antifeminist evangelicals? Evangelical identity, subcultural location, and attitudes toward feminism. *Gender & Society, 18*(4), 451–472.

Gannon, S. (2001). (Re)presenting the collective girl: A poetic approach to a methodological dilemma. *Qualitative Inquiry, 7*(6), 787–800.

Gordon, T., & Lahelma, E. (2003). From ethnography to life history: Tracing transitions of school students. *International Journal of Social Research Methodology, 6*(3), 245–254.

Haraway, D.J. (1988). Situated knowledges: The science question in feminism and the privilege of partial perspective. *Feminist Studies, 14*(3), 575–599.

Haraway, D.J. (2004). *The Haraway reader*. New York: Routledge.

Haug, F. et al. (1987). *Female sexualisation. A collective work of memory*. London: Verso.

Hintsala, M.A., & Kinnunen, M. (Eds.) (2013). *Tuoreet oksat viinipuussa. Vanhoillislestadiolaisuus peilissä* [Reflections on Conservative Laestadianism]. Helsinki: Kirjapaja.

Ihonen, M. (2001). Vaikenevat naiset. Keskustelua naisen paikasta 1800-luvun lestadiolaisuudessa [The silent women. Discussion on women's position in nineteenth century Laestadianism]. *Historiallinen Aikakauskirja, 99*(3), 276–292. Retrieved from http://elektra.helsinki.fi/se/h/0018-2362/99/3/vaikenev.pdf

Joensuu, K. (2016). *The physical, moral and spritiual. A study of vitalist psychology and the philosophy of religion of Lars Levi Laestadius* (Doctoral dissertation). Retrieved from https://lauda.ulapland.fi/bitstream/handle/10024/62809/Joensuu_Kosti_ActaE_205_pdfA.pdf?sequence=2

Kutuniva, M. (2007). Keskusteluja naiseudesta, vanhoillislestadiolaisesta uskosta ja uskonnosta [Discussions on womanhood, Conservative Laestadian faith and religion]. In M. Autti, S. Keskitalo-Foley, P. Naskali, & H. Sinevaara-Niskanen (Eds.), *Kuulumisia—Feministisiä tulkintoja naisten toimijuuksista* (pp. 17–36). Rovaniemi: Lapland University Press.

Laestadius, L.L. (1906/1970). *Huutavan ääni korvessa: valikoima kirjoituksia hengellisestä aikakauslehdestä.* [En ropandes röst i öknen 1852–1854]. [Selected writings of religious quarterly]. (J.F. Hellman, Trans.). Hämeenlinna: Karisto.

Laestadius, L.L. (1968). *Hulluinhuonelainen.* [Dårhushjonet: en blick in nådens ordning] [The madhouse: inmate]. (L. Mustakallio, Trans.). Joensuu: Akateeminen kustannusliike.

Lappalainen, S., Lahelma, E., Hynninen, P., Kankkunen, T., & Tolonen, T. (Eds.). (2007). *Etnografia metodologiana. Lähtökohtana koulutuksen tutkimus* [Ethnography as methodology]. Tampere: Vastapaino.

Lather, P. (1991). *Getting smart. Feminist research and pedagogy within the postmodern.* London: Routledge.

Lee, R.M. (1993). *Doing research on sensitive topics.* London: Sage.

Liamputtong Rice, P. (2000). *Among women and reproduction.* Westport, CT: Bergin and Garvey.

Longman, C. (2007). "Not us, but you have changed!" Discourses of difference and belonging among Haredi women. *Social Compass, 54*(1), 77–95.

MacLure, M. (2013). The wonder of data. *Cultural Studies <=> Critical Methodologies, 13*(4), 228–232.

Mahmood, S. (2012). *The politics of piety. The Islamic revival and the feminist subject.* Princeton, NJ, and Oxford: Princeton University Press.

Manning, E., & Massumi, B. (2014). *Thought in the act. Passages in the ecology of experience.* Minneapolis & London: University of Minnesota Press.

Massumi, B. (2002). *Parables for the virtual.* Durham, NC: Duke University Press.

Massumi, B. (2006). Afterword. Painting: The voice of the grain. In B.L. Ettinger (Ed.), *The matrixial borderspace* (pp. 200,1–212,3). Minneapolis: University of Minnesota Press.

Nissilä, H.L. (2013). Kolonisoitu keho, yhteisöllinen minuus. [Colonised body, collective identity]. In M. Myllykoski & M. Ketola (Eds.), *Lestadiolaisuus tienhaarassa* (pp. 61–69). Helsinki: Vartija. Retrieved from http://www.vartija-lehti.fi/wp-content/uploads/2013/05/vartija-lestadiolaisuus-tienhaarassa.pdf

Nykänen, T. (2012). *Kahden valtakunnan kansalaiset. Vanhoillislestadiolaisuuden poliittinen teologia* [Citizens of two kingdoms. The political theology of Conservative Laestadianism]. Rovaniemi: Lapin yliopistokustannus.

Oinas, E. (2001). *Making sense of the teenage body. Sociological perspectives on girls, changing bodies and knowledge.* Åbo, Finland: Åbo Akademi University Press.

Pylväinen, H. (2012). *We sinners.* New York: Henry Holt and Company.

Pyysiäinen, I. (2004). Corrupt doctrine and doctrinal revival: On the nature and limits of the modes theory. In H. Whitehouse & L.H. Martin (Eds.), *Theorizing religions past: Archaeology, history and cognition* (pp. 173–194). Walnut Creek, CA: Alta Mira Press.

Ramazanoglu, C., & Holland, J. (2002). *Feminist methodology. Challenges and choices.* London: Sage.

Rantala, T. (2018). Artist statement: Maternal attunements. *Studies in the maternal*, *10*(1), 4. http://doi.org/10.16995/sim.253

Rantala, T., & Kuusisto, A. (2013). Examining the researcher's position and methodological and ethical particularities of religion and gender. In K. Tirri & E. Kuusisto (Eds.), *Interaction in educational domains* (pp. 63–73). Rotterdam: Sense Publishers.

Rauhala, P. (2013). *Taivaslaulu*. Helsinki: Gummerus.

Richardson, L. (1994). Writing. A method of inquiry. In N.K. Denzin & Y.S. Lincoln (Eds.), *Handbook of qualitative research* (1st ed., pp. 516–529). Thousand Oaks, CA: Sage.

Skeggs, B. (1997). *Formations of class and gender.* London: Sage.

Skeggs, B. (2004). *Class, self, culture.* London: Routledge.

Stanko, E.A. (1997). "I second that emotion": Reflections on feminism, emotionality, and research on sexual violence. In M.D. Schwartz (Ed.), *Researching sexual violence against women: Methodological and personal perspectives* (pp. 74–85). Thousand Oaks, CA: Sage.

Stoeffler, E.F. (1973). *German pietism during the eighteenth century.* Leiden: E. J. Brill.

St. Pierre, E.A. (1997). Nomadic inquiry in the smooth spaces of the field: A preface. *International Journal of Qualitative Studies in Education*, *10*(3), 365–383.

Suolinna, K., & Sinikara, K. (1986). *Juhonkylä: Tutkimus pohjoissuomalaisesta lestadiolaiskylästä* [Juhonkylä: A study of Laestadian village in northern Finland]. Helsinki: SKS.

Talonen, J. (2001). Lestadiolaisuuden hajaannukset [The schisms of Laestadianism]. In J. Talonen & I. Harjutsalo (Eds.), *Iustitia 14, Suomen Teologisen Instituutin Aikakauskirja* (pp. 11–30). Helsinki: Yliopistopaino.

Toivio, K. (2013). Ehkäisykielto: Omantunnon asia vai ihmisoikeuskysymys [The banning of contraception: A question of conscience or human rights]. In M.A. Hintsala & M. Kinnunen (Eds.), *Tuoreet oksat viinipuussa. Vanhoillislestadiolaisuus peilissä* (pp. 124–144). Helsinki: Kirjapaja.

Tolonen, T., & Palmu, T. (2007). Etnografia, haastattelu ja valta (positiot) [Ethnography, interview and power (positions)]. In S. Lappalainen, E. Lahelma, P. Hynninen, T. Kankkunen, & T. Tolonen (Eds.), *Etnografia metodologiana. Lähtökohtana koulutuksentutkimus* (pp. 89–112). Tampere: Vastapaino.

CHAPTER FOUR

Composing Processual Analysis

EMANCIPATORY PERSPECTIVES SOMETIMES limit our thinking to categories and binaries, preventing the perception of non-normative aspirations as legitimate (see Braidotti & Pisters, 2012). However, open-ended data make it impossible to view aspirations through binaries and prefixed categories, and instead compel a focus on processes in-the-making. To be able to read open-ended data, and to be able to study aspirations and their temporary formations, such as gender and subjectivity, out of their usual categories, requires using poststructuralist analysis to be able to examine the movement in the data.

The concept of desire is especially useful in examining processes that are considered non-normative, subjugated, and reactionary, such as the aspirations of Laestadian women, since as religious women's aspirations, they are seen to follow the laws of the religious movement (see, e.g., Mahmood, 2012; Spivak, 1988). To study the aspirational processes in more detail I employed questions from schizoanalysis, formulated by Gilles Deleuze and Félix Guattari (1983). Schizoanalysis is not simply a method but a fully developed philosophy that shifts the interest from individuals to their processes and desires (see Goodchild, 1996, p. 2), and to lines and mappings (see, e.g., Hickey-Moody & Malins, 2007; Powell-Jones & LeRon Shults, 2016; Renold & Ringrose, 2011; Ringrose, 2011). As its multi-layeredness denotes a flat non-structured network of lines rather than a hierarchical construction, schizoanalysis changes the focus from examining decentered subjects to examining aspirational processes and the movement these create in the data. Therefore, it "undertakes not to represent, interpret or to symbolize, but only to make maps and draw lines" (Deleuze & Guattari, 1987, p. 250).

Through this multi-layeredness it was possible to examine the lines as vectors, paths moving between the points of bodies, affects, enunciations, and perceptions, including disjunctions and knots creating potential variations on the movement itself. Examining the movement of lines enabled the interwoven meshwork of life, our worlds, to exist as discursive and lived, and as social and individual since it brought the affective materiality of our social worlds for examination (see Ingold, 2015, pp. 3–11). In this chapter, the composition of the analysis is opened up and depicted. I begin with defining the concepts, reading the data with the concepts from where I continue to the schizoanalytic questions, assembling the analysis machines, and finally experimenting on data.

4.1. Reading the data with concepts and theories

At the beginning of the analysis process, I experimented with the data in search of appropriate reading. As my interest was in minority women's aspirations I read the data with feminist postcolonial theory (e.g., Ahmed, 1998; Mahmood, 2012; Mohanty, 1984; Spivak, 1988; Minh-ha, 1988) and feminist poststructuralist theory and methodology (e.g., Braidotti, 2003, 2005/2006; Cixous, 1993, 2013; Colebrook, 2000; Davies, 1993, 2000, 2014; Davies & Gannon, 2012; Irigaray, 1977/1985a, 1974/1985b, 1984/1993a, 1993b; Lather, 1991, 2007). To theorize the reproduction and the maternal aspirations I included feminist theory on motherhood to the reading (e.g., Baraitser, 2009; Ettinger, 2006; Stone, 2012; O'Reilly, 2004). To understand the religious premises of the women's accounts I read the data in relation to studies on Laestadianism and Laestadian motherhood (e.g., Kutuniva, 2003, 2007; Nissilä, 2013; Nykänen, 2012; Linjakumpu, 2012).

Becoming and desire.

To be able to read the movement in the data, and to examine the women's identity formations as processes I combined poststructuralist concepts of becoming and desire and the questions from schizoanalysis. I began the analysis with the concept of becoming, which is Deleuze and Guattari's (1987) extension of Michel Foucault's (2005) idea of subjectification. With subjectification Foucault referred to self-constitution of moral being[1] and to religious, Christian, virtuosity, and morality in particular; however, for Deleuze and Guattari "the self [was] only a threshold, a door, a becoming between two multiplicities" from one transformation to another (Deleuze & Guattari, 1987, p. 251). These theories enabled subjectivity to be read as a process which is (re)produced constantly

---
[1] Michel Foucault (2005) used the terms "subject," "subjectivity," and "subjection" in varied ways depending on the context, but he still considered the constitution of the subject as always prior to subjection.

through negotiation. Based on this idea subjectivity can never be fully attained, since a subject is an abstraction, which actualizes only when it is connected to its modalities, such as actions, expressions, or bodies.

In my analysis, the concept of becoming served as a tool to examine the women's processes, which made it possible to speak about a subject without a fixed identity and comprising various processes and dispositions. Here, becoming was about the changing constellations that occasionally materialize as subjects, spaces, enunciations, actions, and artifacts, and the coexisting possibility that is enfolded in all matter and information (Braidotti, 2002; Deleuze & Guattari, 1987). Becoming could also be viewed as a line of flight, movement within, across, and between spaces and structures. These structures and spaces are made of various lines and, thus, understood to be under constant change. For instance, religion or society, as much as they are about established buildings and structured practices, they are also about bodies, expressions, and actions, as there are religious communities made of personal faith and churches that are built to represent that faith. Line of flight could also be seen as the transformational movement within these changing spaces and formations (Deleuze & Guattari, 1987).

At this stage of the analysis, I only had the autobiographical writings as data, which I read with the notion of becoming together with a feminist poststructuralist theory and methodology (i.e., Braidotti, 2002, 2003; Davies, 2000; Davies et al., 2001; Irigaray, 1977/1985a, 1974/1985b, 1984/1993a, 1993b; Smith, 2003; Tamboukou, 2010). The concept of becoming assisted in seeing the movement in the data in the midst of the multi-layered events:

> I got time for the doctor, who thank God, had Laestadian relatives, so she suggested taking the pill to balance the hormones. That time I couldn't agree to take them. I felt it was a sin, but when I was getting worse I was ready... I asked my friends for their opinion on it, and they said it is not acceptable... I went to doctors again. I was asked if I wanted the procedure. Sure, I wanted it... Since then I haven't had a second thought... I was not allowed to get pregnant any more... I was happy with my "destiny."... (Excerpt from the autographical writings data, 2012)

Reading with the concept of becoming highlighted the change in the woman's process but it failed to acknowledge the subtler variations included in these processes; using becoming brought in a leap toward change but did not assist in examining the movement itself. The challenges with the analysis concerned how to approach the intertwined matters such as atmospheres, affects, and bodies within the face-to-face encounters. I was also pondering the question, how to analyze the women's processes within and between the autobiographical texts and as part of the data production and how the various forces function within the women's religious lines.

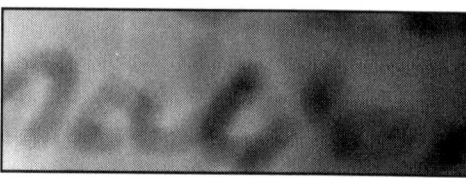

Pic. 4.1.1.
Movement in the text
(Autobiographical writings data, 2012–2013).

Reading the data with feminist theory (e.g., Braidotti, 2003, 2005/2006; Colebrook, 2000; Irigaray, 1977/1985a, 1974/1985b, 1984/1993a, 1993b), specifically feminist theory on female writing (Cixous, 1993, 2013; Kristeva, 1985), made the materiality, the embodied affective intensities of the data, and their intra-active tendencies (see Barad, 2007) resonate:

> I remember being confused about . . . breast growing and hips getting bigger . . . (Excerpt from the collaborative data, 2013)

> I . . . enjoy a warm shower in the middle of the day. (Excerpt from the autobiographical writings data, 2012)

These articulated descriptions of embodied elaborations of emotions were read for their mattering intensities and resonances. As Maggie MacLure (2013) suggests, "there is [. . .] another potentiality associated with data [that] can be felt on occasions where something—perhaps a comment in an interview, or a strange facial expression—seems to reach out from the inert corpus (corpse) of the data to grasp us" (p. 228). These emotions differed from affect in their linearity; they seemed to suspend the nonlinear movement of intensities and enclose them to narrative form. They stopped the movement of intensities as they coded the already felt into experience. To make visible the affective events in the data required breaking and interrupting the flow of the data, since the intensities only appear through interferences, breaks, and cuts, in this linear narrative movement from past to present. This was because intensities, in their nonlinear processes, are virtualities, and only potentials in the present event (Massumi, 2002).

Examining these fluid processes and tracing the intensities, bursts of words, or hesitations, or in animated tones required mapping their movement and drawing lines. This was to bring forth the affects in the women's processes, capturing the forces in their movements (Deleuze, 1995, 1998; Williams, 2013). Thus, the lines could indicate particular intensities in the expressions and articulations, which enabled them to be mapped into a cartography, into mappings of the expressions, the variations in tones and silences. In other words, the women's expressions and articulations were followed in the data to map the movement of their processes, in which they negotiated their desired subjectivity.

The aim of the mapping was to create a drawing of the changing processes, using lines that enabled movement rather than the halting of movement through structures. Mapping connected lines to produce temporary constellations and arrangements. It enabled the otherwise implicit intensities of expressions, tones, and silences to be drawn in the data for examination. These lines are considered cartographical:

> They compose us, as they compose our map ... They have nothing to do with language; it is, on the contrary, language which must follow them. (Deleuze & Guattari, 1987, p. 224)

This is to grasp the interconnective processes within data. The lines are both physical and abstract temporary net-like arrangements, which can form vectors and axioms, or micro modelizations of subjectivity (Guattari, 2013), but the lines also matter (Barad, 2007; Braidotti, 2003). Mattering denotes the situatedness of these temporary processes as the lines are actual and real paths of one's life (Deleuze & Guattari, 1987; Deleuze & Parnet, 2007). The lines are not about articulated or the written enunciations, but about the processes which these articulations follow. So, the aspirational forces are depicted by lines, which are then mapped to make the temporary formations to be perceived and able to matter. This makes them not just articulated aspirations, but aspirations that can produce temporary (social) formations of power such as subjectivities (see Ingold, 2015).

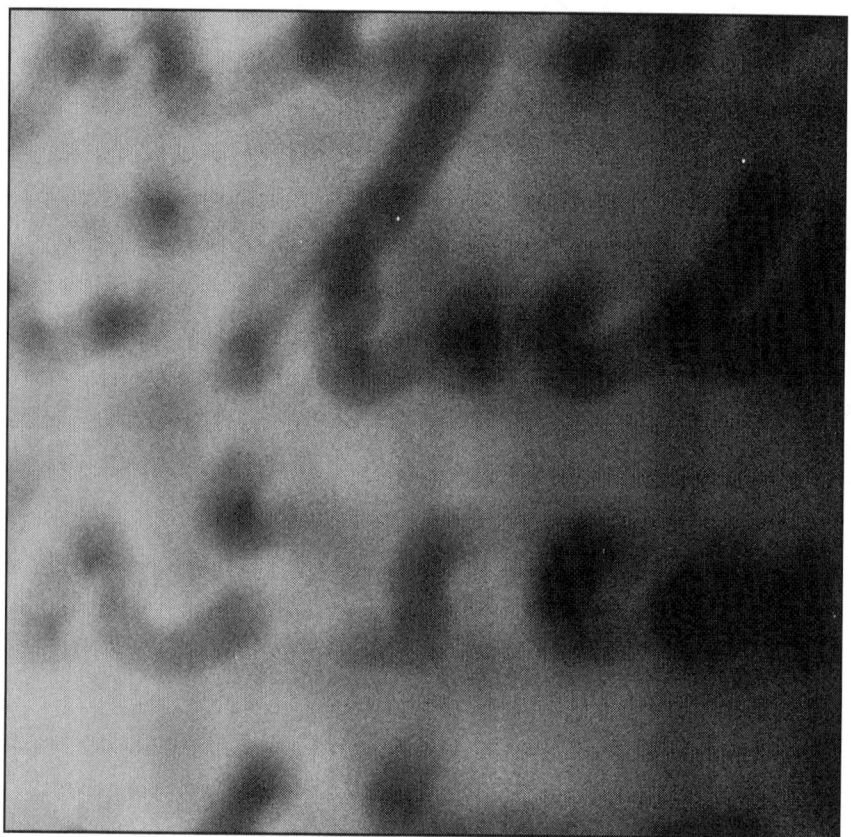

Pic. 4.1.2.
Intensities in the text (Autobiographical writings data, 2012–2013).

Force in the articulations further problematizes the distinction between language and life—the binary between the discursive, the mediated, the felt, and the experienced. Deleuze (1988) writes with Spinoza's (1667/1996) naturalistic ethics that "there is no longer any difference between the concept and life," as for instance, the women's written and orally expressed aspirations are real, which matter and actualize in embodied everyday practices and from there they can further construct collective and communal practices and organizations. This is because affect is the autonomous level where body and mind resonate, co-emerge, and matter as a movement between activity and passivity (Massumi, 2002; see Bergson, 1910/2010; Whitehead, 1978/1985).

The affective movement makes the women's lines to matter to become real with purpose, even though their processes are relational and always dependent and multiple in their productions. Therefore, as the women's processes are situated, they make no sense without their circumstances and milieu, and thereof cannot be examined without their ever-changing contexts. This situatedness and relationality also make it impossible to establish singular entities as individuals or subjects, because there are no individual processes; they are always collective constellations in their situatedness (Haraway, 1988).

These intensities and mattering lines in the data required further examination. The concept of desire proved to have the necessary multidimensionality for examining debated aspirations and allowed including a variety of other theories into the analysis. Since women's identity formation required examining various processes and movement in the data, employing desire enabled me to map these processes for their intensities, depicting the simultaneous movement between religious guidance, one's conscience, and ethics:

> in a way, we are not automatically [guided] that we have our own will, and we choose the path we want to proceed along... I have always had this thought that God gives me the choice and guides me in a certain way, but I choose myself whether I take his advice, and I choose the path I take... but in a way I think, [faith] provides that kind of fundamental trust in life, ... [force that] "carries" me... (Excerpt from the recorded data, 2013)

In this, the concept of desire made more explicit the interconnective lines of everyday life in the women's processes as it assisted in perceiving the social and the natural world as entwined in the articulation of thinking and feeling, the two, which are often understood as separate (see Whitehead, 1978/1985). This enabled the move from common understanding of desire as an individual "need" or a craving, for instance, as the need to consume or to believe, to perceive it as a shared and distributed but also more singular conceptual force-feel arrangement, which does not derive from needs, but instead, the "needs derive from desire" as its counter products (Deleuze & Guattari, 1983, p. 27). Desire is therefore a life force even though it is often experienced as personal (Barad, 2007). This reading of data with desire connected women's aspirations and made them explicit, and ready for further examination with schizoanalytic questions.

4.2. SCHIZOANALYSIS

The concept of desire is central to "schizoanalysis," which Deleuze and Guattari (1983, p. 334) coined to study the collective nature of human activity and the functions of the (post)modern mind. Their interest in desire was the machinic force producing social currents and flows. For them, desire was therefore a force which is neither reigned in nor mastered, as it is neither individual nor outside the subject. It functions like a machine producing the real with relations beyond the social and its signs and meanings. As mentioned earlier, desire can connect semiotic, material, and social forces to form arrangements. Therefore, to create the schizoanalytic machine one needs to connect one's desires into arrangement, and then name these arrangements. In discussing desire and its machinic productions, the concept of arrangement is used here instead of assemblage. Because arrangements allow constant change and thinking beyond entities and systems, they allow for instance, the Laestadian community to be understood as a temporal arrangement of molecular machines engaged together to create lines, productions and antiproductions (see Buchanan, 2015; Culp, 2016). In their complexity as living engagements they only function within the event in which they were assembled.

Schizoanalysis combines two major social theories—Freudian psychoanalysis and Marxist dialectical materialist production—to create a desiring production, critical societal analysis, which uses the Freudian concept of libido and the Marxist concept of labor power as the functions of "desiring machines" (Deleuze & Guattari, 1983, p. 336; Deleuze & Guattari, 1987, pp. 440–441; Goodchild, 1996). A common way of employing schizoanalysis is to use it as a social analysis that works toward a delusion-free understanding of the relation between human and society, and it refers to necessary abnormalities, differences, as productions of the social reality. Unlike this, here the schizoanalysis was used together with the concept of desire to map women's aspirations made within the effects of different social systems, for instance, the state and religion but also the ecological worlds (Deleuze & Guattari, 1983, 1987; Massumi, 1992).

Assembling the desiring machines.

Deleuze and Guattari's (1983) schizomethodology included schizoanalytic questions which were adapted here as tools for reading the data and for assembling the desiring machines. The focus was on the lines and their functions, which the machines produced in the reading. The first four schizoanalytic questions are answered and explained further with illustrations in this chapter, but the remaining five questions are included and explicated with the excerpts from the original data analysis in the next chapter. The first two questions of schizoanalysis were (1) *What are [the] subject's desiring machines* and (2) *What are put into the desiring machines?* These questions concerned the assembly of the desiring machines and the components put into the machines. This required reading the data with the concept of desire and reading the data for its movement, which was demonstrated in the earlier sections of this chapter.

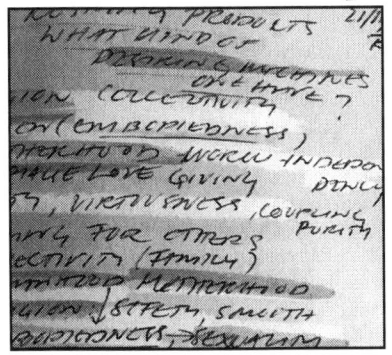

Pic. 4.2.1.
Aspirations in the data
(Notes of the author, 21 November 2014).

With the help of schizoanalytic questions I continued to examine the functions of the women's written and articulated aspirations to interconnect them for analysis. Assembling the connected aspirations and their arrangements into the titled designated desiring machines was one way to study the functions of desire and what it can produce. In the making of a desiring machine there is no wrong or right way (Deleuze & Guattari, 1987), since the arrangements are constantly intersecting with other arrangements and multiplied, traversing to various directions as they are collectively made.

In schizoanalysis these desire forces coming through the machines are examined by mapping them to follow how these forces operate and become shaped by the various other flows, misfires, and currents that they encounter. By mapping the aspirational forces schizoanalysis examines the processes of the social, the psychic, and nature, as Deleuze and Guattari (1987) explain: "Schizoanalysis does not pertain to elements or aggregates, nor to subjects, relations, or structures. It pertains only to lineaments running through groups as well as individuals" (p. 225).

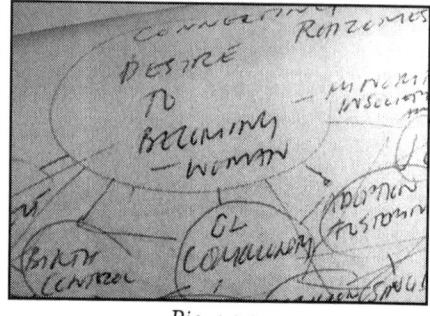

Pic. 4.2.2.
Mapping aspirations for analysis
(Illustration by the author, 28 November 2014).

Desire is the fuel with which the machines and machinic arrangements operate, but to function, desire needs abstract machines, arrangements of enunciations, expressions, and significations. These machines connect to produce lines, but how they succeed always depends on what is put into the machines and the processes and arrangements in which they emerge. Therefore, what was produced with desire was here understood as real within the particular situated process. This real is not universal, since it is only true in and to its own process. For instance, if the women's aspirations were taken out of their context, they would have lost their connective quality through which they function, and through which the aspirations make sense. In other words, the women's aspirations had to be examined in the discussions and written articulations in which they emerged, since the lines that their aspirations could produce or not produce depended on the coding of other articulations, bodies, and practices in the process.

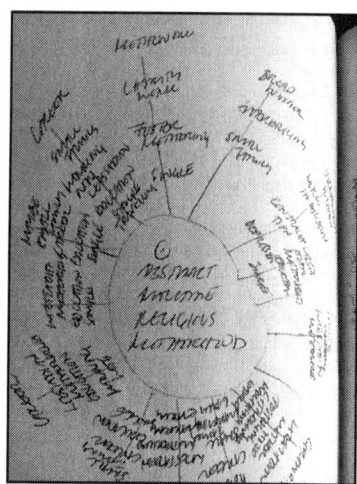

Pic. 4.2.3.
Codings of a desiring machine
(Illustration by the author, 8 March 2015).

Thus, the focus in the reading was on the processes, intensities, and the movements of the data, and on grasping the relationality of the expressions and enunciations, symbolic and bodily, to escape one-sided and subjugating discourses. The lines emanating from the machines were now arranged into well-defined sections to demonstrate how the different machines produced lines within different spheres. This, however, was done only to assist separating the lines for more detailed examination not to situate and categorize them (see Pic. 4.2.8). After this I added various readings to the analysis to be able to examine the entwined and co-productive nature of the analysis. I used the most appropriate layers of each excerpt to be able to bring forth some of the most interesting movements in the data. This enabled the lines to be coded by the various other lines, currents, machines, and spheres through which they had traversed.

The functions of the desiring machines.

The third question (3) *How do they work?* deals with the mechanics of the desiring machine and what actually happens in the desiring process. Desiring machines operate within the social codes, which yet are different in nature and in regime: while the social production is about defining codes and overcoding, the desiring machine is about decoding and deterritorializing (Deleuze & Guattari, 1983). This desire production is always agentic since it is combined and shared; its agency is in the multitude of both folding and unfolding processes and encounters (see also Barad, 2003, 2007; Ettinger, 2005, 2009).

Desire as a life force works everywhere there are processes and life, contrast to the belief that desire would be personal and limited to functions of individual thinking and actions (Goodchild, 1996). Rather, as a connective force it always needs an arrangement to function, and therefore desire is not the intention itself, but the force in the intention. Nor is it an entity, as it can only function and create an arrangement in coalition with other forces. Therefore, it is about co-production; to make one desiring machine requires making another, because none of them

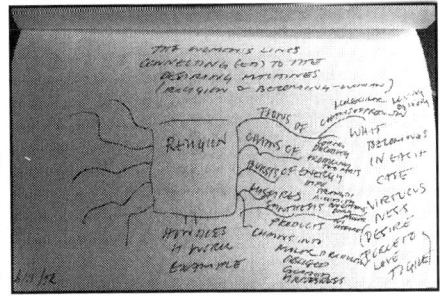

Pic. 4.2.4.
Functions of a religious desiring machine (Illustration by the author, 18 November 2014).

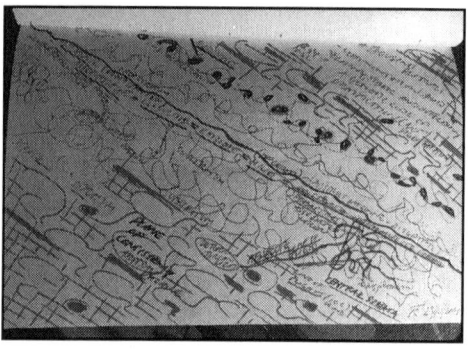

Pic. 4.2.5.
Picturing the stratification of lines
(Deleuze & Guattari, 1987)
(Illustration by the author, 23 October 2014).

could be assembled or function alone. In order for desire to be a force pushing the women's lines in different directions, its elements had to be autonomous, yet inseparable (Deleuze & Guattari, 1983). Machinic in these formations was essential since it explained "subjectivity outside the classical frame of the anthropocentric humanistic subject," as Braidotti (2002, p. 229) explicates. Machinic is the resonances and vibrations, as, for example, the women's paths reveal dynamics of differing, intersecting, and overlapping processes when examined.

The outcomes of schizoanalysis.

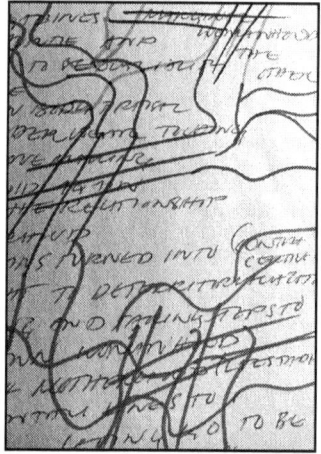

Pic. 4.2.6.
Smooth and striated lines in the analysis (Notes and illustrations by the author, 29 October 2014).

The next question (4) *With what syntheses/outcomes?* addressed the outcomes and processes produced within schizoanalysis. The lines come out of the desiring machines as chained, decoded, and deterritorialized and move within territories, smooth and striated, creating patterns, depending on the spaces they navigate through. As there are different lines, smooth and striated lines, they still entwine as they return to one another and create different movements from one moment to the next (Deleuze & Guattari, 1987). This makes the women's processes different, but not as different from but as different within as the movement within each process changes the process itself.

In this study three machines were assembled: a desiring machine of religion and faith, a desiring machine of collectivity, and a desiring machine of womanhood. There were also other smaller machines working beside these in the experiment. To name a few, there were desiring machines of mothering, sexuality, coupling, as well as work and education, yet these all resonated with desiring machines of religious guidance and virtuousness.

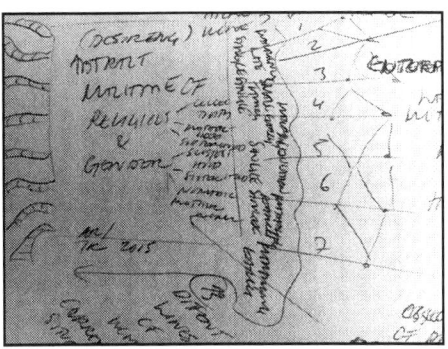

Pic. 4.2.7.
Lines coming out of the desiring machines
(Illustration by the author, 8 March 2015).

But why these machines and none of the others? Choosing these arrangements was not a clear outcome of the analysis, but a result of reading the data continuously with various concepts, theories, and literature for a long time. Finally, the analysis came to a stage at which certain parts of the women's texts began to resonate, which then afforded the reading of the texts with the concept of desire. At the end, most of the lines gathered around faith, collectivity, and womanhood, and therefore I decided to assemble desiring machines of faith (guidance and reasoning), collectivity (coupling, sexuality, and mothering), and womanhood (female and nomadic subjectivity). These were assembled to be able to examine the functions and the processes they produced, in which the women's aspirations were negotiated. Here the three desiring machines worked with their minor machines. Religious machines were assembled with the minor machines of sacred/secular, guidance, reasoning, and contentment, machines of collective desire comprising coupling, sexuality, and realizations of maternal and mothering practices. The machines produced lines, arrangements,

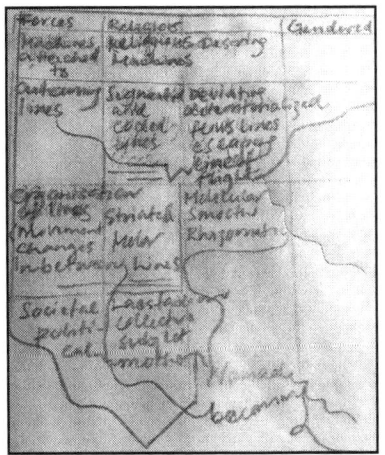

Pic. 4.2.8.
Differenciation and movement of the lines
(Illustration by the author, 11 February 2015).

and foldings as ways of approaching formations and modalities of subjectivity, such as expressions, enunciations, and bodies.

Schizoanalysis was thus about questions, machines, and lines that assisted in mapping the women's processes. The lines gave spatial information about the coordinates, the locations they traversed through, and connections they made with other lines. In the data, these lines were always situated by their arrangements, in which the narratives, stories, and texts could not be separated from their milieus (see Guattari, 2013). However, during the analysis the lines got separated, segmented, entangled, coded, recoded, and overcoded while running through the desiring machines in order to be examined. Through these the women's lines were made explicit in the midst of other arrangements and events.

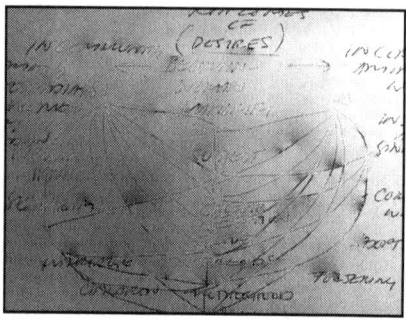

Pic. 4.2.9.
Mappings of the desiring machines produced (Illustrations by the author, 28 November 2014).

The last five questions of schizoanalysis were as follows: What is a burst of energy in the machine? What constitutes misfires? With what chains? With what flows? With what becomings in each case? These questions focus on the outcomes of desiring processes and depict the movement of the lines in the analysis in the next chapter.

References

Data
Writings data, November 2012–April 2013
Recorded data from the face-to-face sessions, 19–20 April 2013 and 29 December 2013

Literature
Ahmed, S. (1998). *Differences that matter. Feminist theory and postmodernism*. Cambridge: Cambridge University Press.
Barad, K. (2003). Posthumanist performativity: Toward an understanding of how matter comes to matter. *Signs: Journal of Women in Culture and Society, 28*(3), 801–831.
Barad, K. (2007). *Meeting the universe halfway: Quantum physics and the entanglement of matter and meaning*. Durham, NC: Duke University Press.
Baraitser, L. (2009). *Maternal encounters: An ethic of interruption*. London and New York: Routledge.
Bergson, H. (1910/2010). *Matter and memory*. (N.M. Paul and W. S. Palmer, Trans.). Digireads.com Publishing.
Braidotti, R. (2002). *Metamorphoses: Towards a materialist theory of becoming*. Cambridge: Polity Press.
Braidotti, R. (2003). Becoming woman: Or sexual difference revisited. *Theory, Culture & Society, 20*(3), 43–64.
Braidotti, R. (2005/2006). Affirming the affirmative: On nomadic affectivity. Rhizomes. *Cultural Studies in Emerging Knowledge*. Issue 11/12. Retrieved from http://www.rhizomes.net/issue11/braidotti.html
Braidotti, R., & Pisters, P. (2012). Introduction. In R. Braidotti & P. Pisters (Eds.), *Revisiting normativity with Deleuze* (pp. 1–8). London: Bloomsbury.
Buchanan, I. (2015). Assemblage theory and its discontents. *Deleuze Studies, 9*(3), 382–392.
Cixous, H. (1993). *Three steps on the ladder of writing*. New York: Columbia University Press.
Cixous, H. (2013). *Meduusan nauru ja muita ironisia kirjoituksia* [Le rire de la Méduse et autres ironies]. (H. Rundgren and A. Sevón, Trans.). Helsinki: Tutkijaliitto.
Colebrook, C. (2000). Introduction. In I. Buchanan & C. Colebrook (Eds.), *Deleuze and feminist theory* (pp. 1–17). Edinburgh University Press.
Culp, A. (2016). *Dark Deleuze*. Minneapolis: University of Minnesota Press.
Davies, B. (1993). *Shards of glass: Children reading and writing beyond gendered identities*. Cresskill, NJ: Hampton Press.
Davies, B. (2000). *A body of writing 1990–1999*. Walnut Creek, CA: Alta Mira Press.
Davies, B. (2014). *Listening to children: Being and becoming*. Abingdon: Routledge.

Davies, B., Dormer, S., Gannon, S., Laws, C., Rocco, S., Lenz Taguchi, H., & McCann, H. (2001). Becoming schoolgirls: The ambivalent project of subjectification. *Gender and Education, 13*(2), 167–182.
Davies, B., & Gannon, S. (2012). Collective biography and the entangled enlivening of being. *International Review of Qualitative Research, 5*(4), 357–376.
Deleuze, G. (1988). *Spinoza: Practical philosophy.* (R. Hurley., Trans.). San Francisco: City Lights Books.
Deleuze, G. (1995). *Negotiations 1972–1990.* (M. Joughin, Trans.). New York: Columbia University Press.
Deleuze, G. (1998). *Essays critical and clinical.* (D.W. Smith & M.A., Trans.) Burchill, London, UK: Verso
Deleuze, G., & Guattari, F. (1983). *Anti-Oedipus: Capitalism and schizophrenia.* (R. Hurley, Trans.) London: Athlone.
Deleuze, G., & Guattari, F. (1987). *A thousand plateaus: Capitalism and schizophrenia.* (B. Massumi, Trans.). Minneapolis: University of Minnesota Press.
Deleuze, G., & Parnet, C. (2007). *Dialogues II.* (H. Tomlinson & B. Habberjam, Trans.). New York: Columbia University Press.
Ettinger, B.L. (2005). Copoiesis. *Framework X Ephemera, 5*(X), 703–713. Retrieved from http://www.ephemerajournal.org/sites/default/files/5-Xettinger.pdf
Ettinger, B.L. (2006). *The matrixial borderspace. (Essays from 1994–1999).* Minneapolis: University of Minnesota Press.
Ettinger, B.L. (2009). *Yhdessätuotanto* [Copoiesis]. Helsinki: Tutkijaliitto.
Foucault, M. (2005). *The hermeneutics of the subject: Lectures at the Collège de France 1981–1982.* (G. Burchell, Trans.). New York: Palgrave MacMillan.
Goodchild, P. (1996). *Deleuze & Guattari: An introduction to the politics of desire.* London: Sage.
Guattari, F. (2013). *Schizoanalytic cartographies.* (A. Coffey, Trans.). London: Bloomsbury.
Haraway, D.J. (1988). Situated knowledges: The science question in feminism and the privilege of partial perspective. *Feminist Studies, 14*(4), 575–599.
Hickey-Moody, A., & Malins, P. (2007). Introduction. In A. Hickey-Moody & P. Malins (Eds.), *Deleuzian encounters: Studies in contemporary social issues* (pp. 1–24). London: Palgrave.
Ingold, T. (2015). *The life of lines.* New York: Routledge.
Irigaray, L. (1977/1985a). *This sex which is not one.* (C. Porter, Trans.). New York: Cornell University Press.
Irigaray, L. (1974/1985b). *Speculum of the other woman.* (G.C. Gill, Trans.). New York: Cornell University Press.
Irigaray, L. (1984/1993a). *An ethics of sexual difference.* (C. Burke & G.C. Gill, Trans.). New York: Cornell University Press.
Irigaray, L. (1993b). *Je, tu, nous.* New York: Routledge.

Kristeva, J. (1985). Stabat mater. The female body in Western culture: Semiotic perspectives. *Poetics Today, 6*(1/2), 133–152. Retrieved from http://www.jstor.org/stable/1772126

Kutuniva, M. (2003). Kaiken se kestää, kaikessa uskoo, kaikessa toivoo, kaiken se kärsii. Katkelmia lestadiolaisäidin elämästä [Fragments of the life of Laestadian mother]. In P. Naskali, M. Autti, S. Keskitalo-Foley, A. Korhonen & M. Kutuniva (Eds.), *Tuulia. Feministisiä näkökulmia lappilaiseen sukupuolikulttuuriin* (pp. 61–80). Rovaniemi: Lapin yliopistopaino.

Kutuniva, M. (2007). Keskusteluja naiseudesta, vanhoillislestadiolaisesta uskosta ja uskonnosta [Discussions on womanhood, Conservative Laestadian faith and religion]. In M. Autti, S. Keskitalo-Foley, P. Naskali & H. Sinevaara-Niskanen (Eds.), *Kuulumisia—Feministisiä tulkintoja naisten toimijuuksista* (pp. 17–36). Rovaniemi: Lapin yliopistopaino.

Lather, P. (1991). *Getting smart. Feminist research and pedagogy within the postmodern.* London: Routledge.

Lather, P. (2007). *Getting lost: Feminist efforts a double(d) science.* Albany: State University of New York Press.

Linjakumpu, A. (2012). *Haavoittunut yhteisö. Hoitokokoukset vanhoillislestadiolaisuudessa* [Pastoral care meetings in Conservative Laestadianism]. Tampere: Vastapaino.

MacLure, M. (2013). The wonder of data. *Cultural Studies <=> Critical Methodologies, 13*(4), 228–232.

Mahmood, S. (2012). *The politics of piety. The Islamic revival and the feminist subject.* Princeton, NJ: Princeton Universtity Press.

Massumi, B. (1992). *User's guide to capitalism and schizophrenia: Deviations from Deleuze and Guattari.* Cambridge, MA: The MIT Press.

Massumi, B. (2002). *Parables for the virtual.* Durham, NC: Duke University Press.

Minh-ha, T. T. (1988). Not you/Like you: Post-colonial women and the interlocking question of identity and difference. *Feminism and the Critique of Colonial Discourse, 3-4,* 71–77. Retrieved from https://culturalstudies.ucsc.edu/inscriptions/volume-34/trinh-t-minh-ha/

Mohanty, C.T. (1984). Under Western eyes: Feminist scholarship and colonial discourses. *Boundary, 2. 12*(3), 333–358. Retrieved from http://www2.kobe-u.ac.jp/~alexroni/IPD%202015%20readings/IPD%202015_5/under-western-eyes.pdf

Nissilä, H-L. (2013). Kolonisoitu keho, yhteisöllinen minuus [Colonized body, collective identity]. In M. Myllykoski & M. Ketola (Eds.), *Lestadiolaisuus tienhaarassa* (pp. 61–69). Helsinki: Vartija. Retrieved from http://www.vartija-lehti.fi/wp-content/uploads/2013/05/vartija-lestadiolaisuus-tienhaarassa.pdf

Nykänen, T. (2012). *Kahden valtakunnan kansalaiset. Vanhoillislestadiolaisuuden poliittinen teologia* [Citizens of two kingdoms: The political theology of Conservative Laestadianism]. Rovaniemi: Lapin yliopistokustannus.

O'Reilly, A. (Ed.). (2004). *From motherhood to mothering: The legacy of Adrienne Rich's Of Woman Born*. Albany State University of New York Press. Ebrary Academic Complete.

Powell-Jones, L., & LeRon Shults, F. (Eds.). (2016). *Deleuze and the schizoanalysis of religion*. London: Bloomsbury.

Renold, E., & Ringrose, J. (2011). Schizoid subjectivities? Re-theorizing teen girls' sexualcultures in an era of "sexualization." *The Australian Sociological Association, 47*(4), 389–409.

Ringrose, J. (2011). Beyond discourse? Using Deleuze and Guattari's schizoanalysis to explore affective assemblages, heterosexually striated space, and lines of flight online and at school. *Educational Philosophy & Theory, 43*(6), 598–618.

Smith, P.M. (2003). *Mapping the whirled. Syncopations in the life of a woman religious*. Melbourne: Spectrum Publications.

Spinoza, B. (1677/1996). *Ethics*. E. Curley (Ed. and Trans.). London: Penguin Books.

Spivak, G. (1988). Can the subaltern speak? In C. Nelson & L. Grossberg (Eds.), *Marxism and the interpretation of culture* (pp. 271–313). London: Macmillan.

Stone, A. (2012). Against matricide: Rethinking subjectivity and the maternal body. *Hypatia, 27*(1), 118–138.

Tamboukou, M. (2010). Charting cartographies of resistance: Lines of flight in women artists' narratives. *Gender and education, 22*(6), 679–696.

Whitehead, A.N. (1978/1985). *Process and reality* (Corrected ed). (D.R. Griffin and D.W. Sherburne, Eds.). New York: The Free Press.

Williams, J. (2013). *Gilles Deleuze's Difference and Repetition. A critical introduction and guide*. Edinburgh: Edinburgh University Press.

CHAPTER FIVE

The Movements of Lines

THESE FOLLOWING THREE chapters present some excerpts of the data analysis, which include data produced in autobiographical and collaborative writing and recorded material of the face-to-face sessions. The analysis is composed by using different theories and studies together with Deleuze and Guattari's (1983, 1987) concept of desire and by following loosely their method of schizoanalysis. Schizoanalytic questions enable a way to follow the movement of data and to map the women's aspirations, the intersective and entangled expressions and articulations, to make sense of these within the same analysis. As the first four questions of schizoanalysis were explained in chapter four, the last five questions were used to examine and describe the movement of the lines in the data as demonstrated in the next three subchapters.

In reading the data with the concept of desire the women's expressions were examined for their affects and intensities. In this analysis, some of the women's expressions responded strongly to the reading, highlighting the intensity of certain expressions. The intensities seemed to function here within "the superlinear, super-abstract realm of potential," which is "asocial, but not presocial—it *includes* social elements" but it mixes and combines them with other "elements according to different logic" (Massumi, 2002, pp. 31, 30; see also Bergson, 1910/2010). In other words, the intensities functioned at emerging levels of tendencies, initial stages of something appearing, in the form of things that can be sensed and felt but not experienced as such. In assembling the desiring machines, these most resonating and accumulated expressions were put into the machines that would then connect them to create cartographic mappings of lines. These lines demonstrated the movement that the women's aspirations produced in an attempt to form temporary arrangements (modalities, e.g., enunciations, practices, bodies, etc. of subjectivity) while still being coded by various other machines.

The following analysis presents the intensities and the resonances of the data, which the different machines produced together, as lines, arrangements, and (un)foldings. The emphasis is on the events in which the course of the lines and their intersections changed or were disrupted. However, to be able to analyze the movement of the lines required exploring articulations together with mechanisms of these machines. This was done with the questions of schizoanalysis, which enabled the lines to be followed, and their various movements and formations to be unfolded. The lines created by these machines are not to be regarded as representations of individuals or their experiences; instead, the lines depict the expressions, articulations, and intensities—the movement in the data—in this particular experimental analysis. The analysis expresses the impersonal relations and resonances between, for instance, forces, images, and temporal dispositions that generate movement and enable the expressions to be mapped. In other words, the desiring machines here depict how the personal, social, and ecological forces are intertwined and involved in the (anti)productions of cartographical lines.

In the original analysis these desiring machines and their submachines created a structure so that the main machines represented the main chapters and the smaller submachines signified the subsections. The first section of the analysis consisted of religious machines working with the minor machines of sacred and secular, devotion, guidance, and contentment. The second section comprised collective machines of relationships, sexuality, and realizations of motherhood. The third section of the analysis included desiring machines of womanhood with femaleness, individuality, and minority, but also folded the analysis sections together. This arrangement brought clarity to the multidimensional and asymmetrical production of the lines and made the analysis possible to follow. The analysis expanded from the beginning toward the end as it began with the processes of faith; continued to the relationships, sexuality, and mothering; and ended at the foldings and unfoldings of subjectivity in order to form an understanding of the women's subjectivity formation process. The productions became more intensified and entwined toward the end where they all encountered and overlapped with different aspects of Laestadian female subjectivity. Separating the main desiring machines into three individual chapters allowed each machine, their submachines, and productions to be developed further while they also created multiple layers to the analysis.

Here, however, I decided to proceed differently in order to focus on the movement in the data and bring attention to the various flows, disturbances, and breaks occurring in the data. Therefore, the focus is on the schizoanalytic questions and the intensities and affects these bring forth in the data. This attention on the movement in the data makes explicit the intertwined nature of the women's processes and the differences within the women's aspirations but also allows the data to evolve in more or less non-structured ways. This depicts the messiness and the confused and unlinear nature of the data and its analysis, producing an understanding of the analysis as a less linear, open-ended, and more chaotic, experimental, and muddled exercise. Furthermore, this also manages to stress the differences within the collective data production and similarly the differences within the women's aspirations and their processes. The purpose of examining the affects and intensities in the data was to make sense of the seemingly contradictory expressions and articulations of the women. To be able to make sense of these required understanding the affects and intensities, the movements and events present in the production of the data. Examining the lines that the women's aspirations created made them situated and therefore possible to understand.

The schizoanalytic questions are organized in three subsections, which each sketch the movement and its eruptions in the data. The first subsection examines the flows in the data, the next the disturbances and breaks in the flow, and the last analyzes the temporary chains and formations that emerge in the movement of the data. The excerpts in the analysis have been taken from the written data and transcribed articulations of recorded data, but the excerpts from the original analysis have been modified by removing some of the in-text references to make the movement in the data easier to read and to follow. To conceal the women's identities required disrupting the connection between the women and the texts by using more pseudonyms than there were women. In the analysis, I used ellipses to signify the text that has been removed from the sentence or from the paragraph. Text inside brackets was added to assist the reader to make sense of the content without reciting the entire paragraph or discussion in the analysis.

5.1. Flowing lines

With what (kind of) flows?
Data analysis description/storylines:
The lines start from the women's aspirations, their lives, connections, and communities. Laestadian women are religious and living within religious

devotion; however, the women are not impeded from aspiring and negotiating their faith and identity within their experiences. These women's lines are situated, relational, and collective, but also differing:

> Riina: Life is not in our hands, and I don't want to even imagine what it would be like [if it was]. I don't mean that I don't have any part in it. But even if we plan everything, live [morally] "well," and make the "right" choices, even then, anything can happen.
>
> Sisko: I feel that the things just come to me . . . I often wonder how I should make the decision . . . of course I make the decision . . . I talk to my husband and friends . . . but in a way I feel that certain things just happen. (Recorded data, 2013)

These religious spaces are made of different lines, arrangements, and structures, which are all produced by faith, the religious desiring machines, but as these machines are assembled with the women's aspirations (entangled with other, e.g., social processes): they are subject to change. The next flow coming out starts a new line. . . .

> Riina: In a way, we are not automatically [guided] that we have our own will, and we choose the path we want to proceed along . . . I have always had this thought that God gives me the choice and guides me in a certain way, but I choose myself whether I take his advice, and I choose the path I take . . . but in a way I think, [faith] provides that kind of fundamental trust in life . . . at the bottom that [force] "carries" me . . . faith gives me courage to do things. (Recorded data, 2013)

The women's lines come to an end inside the Laestadian religious order and seem to lead to its paradox; you are free to live your life as you want, yet, at the same time, you want to be guided and as you want to be guided, you need to follow and desire the things that help you to remain guided. Even though these lines form faith as personal relation the lines seem to remain within the external moral rules:

> Riina: If I thought that faith was all about the things that are sinful (not allowed) [and] just there to stop me from doing something, I cannot do this and that . . . no . . . I understand it so that every individual creates their own relationship to things, [but] there is still . . . your own understanding of the way life should be lived. (Recorded data, 2013)

This current is intensely coded by the religious doctrine giving the exact instructions about how to live your life, leaving very little room for interpretation and alternative aspirations. However, the strict coding is interrupted by expression of one's will:

> Sisko: It should be all about what I want [within my faith] not what I am allowed to want.
>
> Riina: We call it "law-guided spirituality" . . . when the rules are more important than the will [of a person]. (Recorded data, 2013)

Some of the lines are overcoded now with these rules stopping the movement of the lines, but the articulation breaks down the coded arrangements. This puts everyone's lines at a halt for a moment until the next current comes in breaking the silence. Questions about the possibility and relation of the communal formations and the singular lines appear as deviations of the molar structured lines become temporarily stronger in the group. These all intertwine at the end and enable the existence of differentiating lines within.

What is a burst of energy in the machine?
Data analysis description/storylines:

Religion can be seen a collective creation, which has power over its members and therefore manages to shape their personal relation to faith, which sometimes results as collective understanding of the teachings and as community up to a certain point. However, as religion and faith are social productions, they also require the existence of bodies to worship collective rules (Deleuze & Guattari, 1987). What becomes interesting here is the notion of ethics and how to function within one's limits, if, for instance, everything from thoughts to practices are at the same time both communal and personal:

> Riina: It is important to know how to function within one's limits... if I don't have experience of something... I cannot judge... I cannot have an opinion on it.

> Sisko: Whatever decisions you make, in a way they are your decisions ... it is your own will. (Recorded data, 2013)

The prevailing collective power is explicitly hovering above, yet there seems to be trouble in identifying it even if it is personally felt and thought and it seems to affect how one understands one's limits and the personal ethics and responsibility of one's choices. However, as remarked above, experience is the key to understanding since judging occurs only in cases where there is no immediate experience available and the mind has to define something based on the idea of it (e.g., Deleuze, 1998; Whitehead, 1978/1985). The next outburst of experience is powerful, as it now turns the brief flow into a molar tight current again pushing toward contentment:

> Ella: [My belief] comes from my experience ... well ... we had the first child, then the second one died, then we had two miscarriages ... I gave birth to a dead fetus ... I remember I was in shock, because I had always wished for big family ... but I prayed that I could be content with the things I have ... In a way, being content ... is to trust that everything will turn out well at the end ... even though things didn't go as ... wanted. (Autobiographical writings data, 2012–2013)

Despite these moments of sorrow and deep disappointment in the body failing to deliver and the tiredness of going through the unbearable mental and bodily strain, the wish to be content persists. The devoutness sends her lines to the striated space of a pious member as she wants a family as well as to be good Laestadian. Her lines could be seen to work in the "process" which "is the becoming of experience" as her thinking and feeling are turned into a belief and belonging into the community (Whitehead, 1978/1985, p. 166). This brings her lines to be articulated in the act of prayer, which is experienced by others in the community, making this community matter as a group, communion, and established structure (see Barad, 2003).

5.2. Breaks in the flow: Relational and sexual configurations

What constitutes misfires?
Data analysis description/storylines:
Singular lines shift the movement toward decoding, deterritorialization, free from the striated aims of Laestadianism, which employs sexuality only for conceiving new life. The lines coming out of desiring machines are transformed as they move from one territory to another; here they move from faith and religious teachings to personal needs:

> Emma: I often thought that I would not get married. And yet my body felt attracted and drawn and needy. [I wondered] how could I manage without [sex] since it felt so good. (Autobiographical writings data, 2012–2013)

The transformation here is initially invisible, but to know Emma's situation as a Laestadian young woman who wanted to belong to the movement, but who also dreamed about single living without marital and family life, is already very modern. Still, to dream about sex outside the marital relationship and without the aim to conceive new life is a transformative action for her as a Laestadian woman to take. However, through the daydreaming she is able to be a sexual being, which transforms her paths and changes their orientation toward her own sustenance. Sexuality is sinful as it is leading to the danger of losing one's virtuousness in the attraction to the opposite sex and moving away from the community. Similarly, in the Oedipal order, these lines remain caught up in desires shaped by expectation of (Western) heterosexual and (nuclear) familial desires (Beckman, 2011). Nevertheless, Emma's lines seem still open for change and movement, and therefore they easily fold together with other lines, even these molar lines of Laestadian pious order.

Despite the sexual forces, desire is not to be regarded as altogether sexual or only as sexual drive heading toward single-minded fulfillment of sexual desire. It does not follow its common understanding as a Freudian libido, in which sexual energy is the product of heterosexual desire produced in the consciousness or the reproduction of it produced in the realm of the nuclear family (Flax, 1990; Deleuze & Guattari, 1983). Therefore, Emma's desire to be physically close to someone is a sexual desire, a yearning or need to be fulfilled, which is different from the force of desire, something non-intentional and non-object-driven.

Still, sexual desire is one of the most important forces in terms of sustenance. Sexuality operates as a (un)productive dimension connecting consciousness with machinic forces in order to actualize as a living arrangement, here as a body. According to Deleuze (2004, p. 254), "the sexual surface is an intermediary between physical depth and metaphysical surface," providing that the release of sexuality from domestic affairs "coincides with the release of the thought from its transcendent determinants" (Beckman, 2011, p. 7). The human body is the machinic arrangement that enables us to desire. Thus, the subject is only part of the production of the body as the human body is a stratum on its own abstraction, a singularity of gathering, thickening process of formation (Deleuze & Guattari, 1987). This is to say that the Laestadian body is not governed by the converted pious heart and soul but is actually the immanent arrangement of forces. In other words, the Laestadian secular body machine, which emits sinful passions, cannot be silenced, since it lacks a ruler for the converted soul as well as for the rational consciousness. Rather, the body is itself a machine and the immanent precursor of the forces that operate with the images, enunciations, and practices in the consciousness.

Next lines go through deterritorialization, transformation. The lines flow following the strong current from the desiring machines, which produce them to flee free for a moment from striated and constructed aims of the community and employing sexuality and sex only for conceiving new life. Singular lines shift the flow into decoding and deterritorialization, which enables the lines to move from one band to another (see Pic. 4.2.5, Deleuze & Guattari, 1987):

> Kerttu: . . . by myself I often admired my breasts in the mirror and enjoyed my body . . . didn't touch myself . . . (Autobiographical writings data, 2012–2013)

The body is needed here to knit together the relations(hip) between forces, images, and temporal dispositions, and to express the movement of the differing forces pushing the lines to connect and produce (Braidotti, 2005/2006). The machinic forces in the body send the lines to decode the molar and structured strata, as Viivi's admiration of her own body, the embodied joy of the physical intimacy, interrupts the pre-ordered lines of Laestadian community law and rules in which sex is strictly reserved for maintaining the sacred order of the community by conceiving new life.

In the fear of sin of opposing the sacred marital intimacy, Leila's lines are coded with pious aims and marital arrangements, but the lines differ as some head toward the structured territory of Laestadian rules while others flee toward alternative arrangements:

> Leila: When living as a single person most problems are related to sexuality. That causes anxiety; what if I never find a spouse? (Autobiographical writings data, 2012–2013)

Some of the women's lines attempt to create a smooth space inside the otherwise striated territory and the obligation to have a spouse and a family to be able to express one's sexuality. Despite the tensions and anxieties, subtle flows arrive to create a movement of affection:

> Silja: It was just unbelievable to fall in love ... at the same time get to know my sexuality and the female side of me ... It was sometimes difficult for my husband to understand how hard it is for a [Laestadian] woman to free herself from (pious) virtuousness! (Autobiographical writings data, 2012–2013)

In the encounter of religious order, social expectations, and sexual needs, the lines are less constrained by the conventional family structure and the taboos of Laestadian sexuality. Although they still seem to struggle to encounter sexuality beyond the stratified territory of rules, virtuousness, and the purpose of conceiving, floods of sexual needs bring lines that aim to secure the sustenance of the bond between a man and a woman and to keep their relationship strong under the strain of having a large family. There are also loops of wants and wishes in the lines—knots of attachment, which are waiting to be articulated. The machinic in the body brings these passions and intensities to matter as the resonances, vibrations, affects, and atmospheres form connections. Desiring coupling and sexuality make interweaving lines, which enable the existence of families and children, as a sign of embodiment, actualization, continuation, and extension of the sacred community. The community, which is protected by the nuclear family circle and realm, creates sexuality as a sinful drive leading to destruction, but it also gives sexuality a significance: it is the machinic energy connecting the couples and pushing them to form the Laestadian sacred cluster, a family with many children. There energy flows from singular lines to communal and marital and further to create the Conservative Laestadian communities.

5.3. Temporary formations

With what chains?

Data analysis description/storylines:

Desiring machines work on discursive flows and bursts of energy, misfires, and syntheses, but also on chains, producing new lines (Deleuze & Guattari, 1983). Motherhood, even if seen as reproductive, also forms chains, loops, and successive lines outside the patriarchal order, lines that become embodied, enfolding this chain into its own special sphere. In motherhood, the smooth and striated encounter each other; the striated line is the need to reproduce, and the smooth is to follow the guidance and trust. Reproductional aims produce the collective as a territory of little change and fluctuation. However tight and ruled the territory seems, there is always some movement and change, since there are both structured and less structured lines and forces functioning together:

> Viivi: Those moments come to my mind, when I dreamed about being pregnant . . . In my mind, I was so ready to be a mother. (Autobiographical writings data, 2012–2013)

Viivi's desire to mother and to be a mother enters novel territory, which could be called maternal. This is the embodied force that is operating to produce lines, which become concrete in the mother-child dyad as two subjectivities together forming an arrangement. The new line connects forces and resonances as they reach the female body, and its plasticity, mucous enterprise, which often successfully receives the other, here the fetus, to entail it into itself, nesting it into its own folding (Irigaray, 1993). But the body is also the point at which the lines matter, to become concrete and visible:

> Viivi: I hoped the first pregnancy will soon be visible.
> (Autobiographical writings data, 2012–2013)

Pregnancy is the visible sign of receiving the other, to connect to the m(other) as other and it is not only an embodied connection, but it is fusion at the level of affect and (un)conscious (Ettinger 2006b). This is the collective subject in which the maternal is machinic: the forces link the embodied lines under its intra-active energies and commands (Braidotti, 2005/2006). Pregnancy offers an interplanetary space for the desire to matter as it is explicit in this expression. Pregnancy is thereof not merely an implication of true faith or loyalty to the communal laws, but a co-production of the social and faith in mother-fetus-procreational dyads:

> Viivi: At the beginning of each new pregnancy or in the case of labor I have felt very strongly that I was doing my duty as a woman for God. (Autobiographical writings data, 2012–2013)

These lines are particularly worthy in the eyes of the community, as the faith is placed in the sacred community, not in the individual itself (Leivo, 2001). The lines vary from following pre-ordered paths to the conscious actions, when the hope of getting pregnant changes into a fear of another pregnancy:

> Viivi: When the fear of getting pregnant was not there, something, some part of me was relieved. Still, I was really scared that someone would notice that I was using something and so I was living kind of double lives. I was not confident with it. I was afraid that I would reveal myself. I wanted to be a good believer and go to heaven. I was really struggling with this. (Autobiographical writings data, 2012–2013)

The lines are coded with virtuousness and rigid obedience to the community rules. Community is the territory of the collective loving, caring, and being cared for, but also the territory that requires compliance to its lines of caring. Her lines struggle in that pastoral governance, as the pain of sharing the maternal space, the womb, with the community in order to become a legitimate female subject takes its toll. So, joy is felt and expressed in the event of miscarriage as it frees the body again from this religious governing. This event in Viivi's memory brings in the unborn fetus as well as the feelings of loss and expectations of her mother's own miscarriages:

> Viivi: The pregnancy ended in miscarriage in week 10. I was relieved and happy . . . At that moment, it was so welcomed. When I went to hospital to have a scan they said it [the fetus] was still there. I almost screamed! It wasn't alive, but still in me . . . Mother was crying her own pain [of miscarriages]. (Autobiographical writings data, 2012–2013)

The pain of having the unwanted, now lifeless fetus taking place in the body, and her mother's agony with her made her lines to escape the Laestadian maternal norm of successive pregnancies and childbirths. However, as she was released from these expectations, her mother's agony over the lost opportunity to live the Laestadian norm surfaced in the event. These lines were heavy from coding, but among these Viivi found strength to sustain (see Deleuze & Parnet, 2007):

> Viivi: I got time for the doctor, who . . . suggested taking the pill . . . That time I couldn't agree to take them . . . I asked my friends for their opinion on it, and they said it is not acceptable . . . I went to doctors again. I was asked if I wanted the procedure. I wanted it . . . I was not allowed to get pregnant any more . . . I was happy with my "destiny." (Autobiographical writings data, 2012–2013)

Balancing her lines between being guided and making decisions was difficult as it meant carrying the burden of sin and blame in the eyes of community. Questioning the sacred order and resisting it was dangerous, as it could result in being excluded from the community and the safety of family and friends:

> Viivi: With a caution I write that I regard my motherhood as being a burden in my life ... it has been a stony and heavy path to travel ... (Autobiographical writings data, 2012–2013)

Acknowledging the high price that was paid to live up to the set expectations of the Laestadian female norm, but also bearing the shame that came from not following the religious order created another path. Her lines no longer echoed the Laestadian female norm as much as they echoed the desired future subjectivity that was yet unknown (Davies, 2014):

> Viivi: Growing up to be a woman has led to pain and sorrow, even tears sometimes. Gradually I am beginning to get to know myself. I am also getting to know my body. Usually, the Laestadian mother is in "shipshape" condition and she looks after herself, in ways that I have also felt to be different. Feeling good [about yourself] is something else ... I am grateful that I have survived these very difficult and "hazy" times of becoming a woman. It left me scarred, but the scars are not all that bad. I have had the strength to ask for help and I have received it. I wish my mother could have done the same. (Autobiographical writings data, 2012–2013)

Even though these lines were transformed, they were still Laestadian, collective, and situated, as the encounters between the generations keep us re-attuned and affectively connected to one another (Ettinger, 1992, 2005, 2006a, 2009). These passages produce transformations, circulations, and sharings and allow moving between the past, present, and future (Ettinger, 2006a, 2009). Within these lines, motherhood is considered a relational process, which resonates the co-constitution of the subjectivity always as enlarged, including more than one and the other.

With what becomings in each case?

The concept of desire is significant for studying fluid constellations such as subjectivity and gender, since it allows examining them outside their usual categories as becoming. Becoming is the process of constant differenciation occurring within the material, symbolic, and discursive effects of life, as Braidotti (2002) further clarifies: "[It] is the actualization of the immanent encounter between subjects, entities and forces which are apt mutually to affect and exchange" (p. 68; see also Deleuze & Guattari, 1987). For a female subject, becoming is not about becoming a woman per se; instead, it is to transform through many flows, currents, governing structures, and relations (see Stagoll, 2010). Through the series of events, in which the past is not separated from the present and future, it constitutes our perception of ourselves as unified subjects.

Data analysis description/storylines:

When Laestadianism is discussed in the media, it is often considered to consist of small identical congregations, limiting the perception of its members and communities as changing:

> Pinja: In the eyes of some outsider (non-Laestadian) and the media my precious and unique life is classified as being the same as any other person's, who happen to believe the same way. (Autobiographical writings data, 2012–2013)

Understanding these groups as fluctuating arrangements of lines, enunciations, interactions, events, and affects enables the lines to be perceived as differing and changing, as Pinja suggests. The differing lines are the less confined and structured lines, which here comprised intensities and connections that operate with all sorts of drives and forces (Deleuze & Guattari, 1983; see also Buchanan, 2008). These lines can create ruptions to the movement through which differing constellations occasionally materialize as subjects (Deleuze & Guattari, 1987; Grosz, 1999).

The lines that do not follow the traditional Laestadian norm of finding a spouse and getting married young are seen as singular. These lines are often interpreted as independent and emerging as a result of rationalizing and individualizing decisions. Nevertheless, a singular is always more than a line; it belongs to a pack and an arrangement of lines from which it cannot be separated (Manning, 2013; cf. Nancy, 2000). However, there are lines that are nomadic, suggesting here the possibility of embodying the decentered routes one's lines take (Braidotti, 1994, 2006, 2011a, 2011b):

> Valma: Growing up in the community that is very conservative in its values and way of life is both a gift and a burden: On one hand, I have a ready female model to grow up into, and principles that help the choices in life and as well as the safe close community, which is invaluable for the growing children and teenagers! On the other hand, when you become "a female subject" you will realize how many beautiful things are twisted to be quite the opposite, difficult, if not impossible... (Autobiographical writings data, 2012–2013)

Valma's lines are struggling within the smooth and striated realms of the community as, on one hand, it seems to offer security but, on the other hand, it seems to dictate and limit the young women's future by requesting them to settle for its reproductive aims (see Alasuutari, 1992; Chodorow, 1978; Friedan, 1963; Ihonen, 1999, 2001; Kutuniva, 2007):

> Valma: On the other hand, I realize that not all the women in society plan to have a career, but in a Conservative Laestadian community, housewifery is such a strong norm that the women who manage to "escape" it are overlooked and marginalized. It is possible to discuss these in the community, but still the community has very strict rules about how to approach and articulate these things as the pastoral discourse always come back to the same point: these principles are accepted and found good in the community. (Autobiographical writings data, 2012–2013)

This religious territory is seen comprising striated and smooth intertwined realms (see Hickey-Moody & Malins, 2007; Malins, 2007), yet at the same time social space is perceived rather differently as the female subject seems to be folded within the molar structures of society, which do not, however, ordain the way a young woman should be, nor do they offer support or security. The religious and social here are the binary realms, in which the women's lines are mapped at the same time:

> Valma: It is exciting to be part of "two worlds" as a woman; to be part of a postmodern whatever-culture and part of a community,

which supports the traditional image of womanhood, and which is now gradually changing. I hope that [in the future] I will not see it as impossible to belong to this community... I am thankful for my siblings and I am worried that I am not offering the same to my own children... I feel that I have a calling elsewhere... I feel that it would be impossible as the mother of a large family. (Autobiographical writings data, 2012–2013)

These lines do not flow freely in the midst of different worlds, the Laestadian communities and the postmodern culture of Finnish society, but they struggle in between these problematic and dictating realms. Belonging to the Laestadian movement in the future seems unsure, however, even though her lines are altered concurrently by religiosity, collectivity, and womanhood; the sacred and secular are separated binaries of traditional and postmodern spheres, making the female subject both a virtuous mother and server of the community, as well as a sexual object and subject. Still, the lines move toward nomadity, not necessarily to escape the often dictating and striated realms, but to aim to transform the realms from within, or at least to shake their structured arrangements.

5.4. Brief summary on the lines

In the previous subchapters the schizoanalytic questions assisted in unfolding the women's lines and their movement, intensities, and affects to examine them in the intersections of Laestadian women's faith, collectivity, and desired subjectivities. The lines depicted the processes of the psyche, the social (or socius) and nature (see Guattari 1989, p.34), within which the women's connections to various social discourses, encounters, religious teachings, communities, and other believers were temporarily formed. The women's lines were constantly coded and decoded by governing laws of society and the limitations of religion, but they still kept constantly becoming something else, as these lines could form various flows within (Deleuze & Guattari, 1987). Faith comprised personal connections to teachings and practices besides the communal and shared understanding of these, making it both a molecular and molar arrangement, simultaneously governing and forming the lines. Faith was produced through believing, although the lines were coded by transcendental powers and religious guidance believed to be outside the subject and its powers (Deleuze & Guattari, 1987; Deleuze & Parnet, 2007; Smith, 2001).

Because desire was understood as an immanent force, which is not human by origin and cannot be produced as such, it can attract abstract forms and values into the desire production. The abstractions were not its own products since the real in desire refers to existence without mediation (Goodchild, 1996), and thus, only the real in desire creates connections, which move in, between, and out of these structures while transforming them. As an arrangement desire "take[s] the entire surroundings that it traverses, the vibrations and flows of every sort to which it is joined," as Deleuze and Guattari (1983, p. 292) attempt to clarify, understanding desiring production as fragmented, comprising a multiple of little machines, parts, and flows that work together. Looking at the data, this meant understanding the situated relationality of the women's lines, as they only make sense in their situated processes; in other words, they have no meaning or movement without the pack. Here for instance, there is no religion or society without their members, citizens, and their actual situated and ecological processes.

However, the women's situated processes included also nomadic lines, which did not start from the religious molar structures, but from the margins of the religious community and movement, making possible the lines to take directions other than the rigid centers, and giving them more freedom from the control of the society and religious movement. Therefore, as the Laestadian women claimed an identity—for instance, the identity of a mother, woman, or subject—they claimed all these identities from the position of a minority. These women were not only minorities as women and religious women in the society, but minority as women in their own community and movement. Thus, this minority becoming functioned as a threshold, an intermediate space, for the women to orient their lines away from the subjugating patriarchal power centers, and map out their routes within but also beyond these minority positions.

Subsequently, for these women, who seemed placed outside the humanist agentic subjecthood for their religiousness, often their lines were escaping the normative Laestadian paths. For instance, one route was through becoming-woman, which was not understood as another form of becoming a minority, but as the necessary starting point for any process of claiming identity (Braidotti, 2005). This claim Braidotti (2003) further explains, that "the reference to 'woman' in the process of 'becoming-woman,' however, does not refer to empirical females, but rather to socio-symbolic constructions, topological positions, degrees, and levels of intensity, affective states" (p. 49). In other words, when the Laestadian women claimed to be women, they automatically claimed the position of a woman, which is not to be understood as positioning themselves as such, but being temporarily that much of an entity to be able to negotiate the points their lines traverse and resist and create diverting lines within (e.g., Mahmood, 2012).

References

Data
Writings data, November 2012–April 2013
Recorded data from the face-to-face sessions, 19–20 April 2013 and 29 December 2013
Collaborative writing data, February 2013–January 2016

Literature
Alasuutari, P. (1992). Ehkäisyn kiellon synty ja umpikuja vanhoillislestadiolaisessa herätysliikkeessä [The origin and the deadlock of the birth control debate in Conservative Laestadianism]. *Sosiologia, 2*, 106–115.
Barad, K. (2003). Posthumanist performativity: Toward an understanding of how matter comes to matter. *Signs: Journal of Women in Culture and Society, 28*(3), 801–831.
Beckman, F. (2011). Introduction: What is sex? An introduction to the sexual philosophy of Gilles Deleuze. In F. Beckman (Ed.), *Deleuze and sex* (pp. 2–29). Edinburgh: Edinburgh University Press.
Bergson, H. (1910/2010). *Matter and memory* (N.M. Paul and W. S. Palmer, Trans.). Digireads.com Publishing.
Braidotti, R. (1994). *Nomadic subjects: Embodiment and sexual difference in contemporary feminist thought.* New York: Columbia University Press.
Braidotti, R. (2002). *Metamorphoses: Towards a materialist theory of becoming.* Cambridge: Polity Press.
Braidotti, R. (2003). Becoming woman: Or sexual difference revisited. *Theory, Culture & Society, 20*(3), 43–64.
Braidotti, R. (2005). A critical cartography of feminist post-postmodernism. *Australian Feminist Studies, (20)* 47, 169–180. http://doi.org/10.1080/08164640500090319
Braidotti, R. (2005/2006). Affirming the affirmative: On nomadic affectivity. *Rhizomes. Cultural studies in emerging knowledge. Issue 11/12.* Retrieved from http://www.rhizomes.net/issue11/braidotti.html
Braidotti, R. (2006). *Transpositions. On nomadic ethics.* Cambridge: Polity Press.

Braidotti, R. (2011a). *Nomadic subjects. Embodiment and sexual difference in contemporary feminist theory*. New York: Columbia University Press.

Braidotti, R. (2011b). The new activism: A plea for affirmative ethics. In L. De Cauter, R. De Roo, & K. Vanhaesebrouck (Eds.), *Art and activism in the age of globalization* (pp. 264–270). Rotterdam: Nai Publishers.

Buchanan, I. (2008). *Deleuze and Guattari's anti-Oedipus*. London: Continuum.

Chodorow, N. (1978). *The reproduction of mothering: Psychoanalysis and the sociology of gender*. Berkeley: University of California Press.

Davies, B. (2014). *Listening to children: Being and becoming*. Abingdon: Routledge.

Deleuze, G. (1998). *Essays critical and clinical*. (D.W. Smith & M.A. Greco, Trans.). Burchill, London, UK: Verso

Deleuze, G. (2004). *The logic of sense*. (M. Lester and C. Stivale, Trans.). London: Continuum.

Deleuze, G., & Guattari, F. (1983). *Anti-Oedipus: Capitalism and schizophrenia*. (R. Hurley, M. Seem & H.R. Lane, Trans.). London: Athlone.

Deleuze, G., & Guattari, F. (1987). *A thousand plateaus: Capitalism and schizophrenia*. (B. Massumi, Trans.). Minneapolis: University of Minnesota Press.

Deleuze, G., & Parnet, C. (2007). *Dialogues II*. (H. Tomlinson & B. Habberjam, Trans.). New York: Columbia University Press.

Ettinger, B.L. (1992). Matrix and metramorphosis. *Differences: A Journal of Feminist Cultural Studies, 4*(3), 176–208.

Ettinger, B.L. (2005). Copoiesis. *Framework X Ephemera, 5*(X), 703–713. Retrieved from http://www.ephemerajournal.org/sites/default/files/5-Xettinger.pdf

Ettinger, B.L. (2006a). *The matrixial borderspace: Essays from 1994–1999*. Minneapolis: University of Minnesota Press.

Ettinger, B.L. (2006b). Matrixial trans-subjectivity. *Theory, Culture & Society, 23*(2–3), 218–222.

Ettinger, B.L. (2009). *Yhdessätuotanto* [Copoiesis]. Helsinki: Tutkijaliitto.

Flax, J. (1990). *Thinking fragments. Psychoanalysis, feminism, and postmodernism in the contemporary West*. Berkeley: University of California Press.

Friedan, B. (1963). *Feminine mystique*. UK: Penquin Books.

Goodchild, P. (1996). *Deleuze & Guattari: An introduction to the politics of desire*. London: Sage.

Grosz, E. (1999). Becoming... An introduction. In E. Grosz (Ed.), *Explorations in time, memory, and futures* (pp. 1–12). Ithaca, NY, and London: Cornell University Press.

Guattari, F. (1989). The three ecologies. (C. Turner, Trans.). *New formations 8,* 131–147.

Hickey-Moody, A., & Malins, P. (2007). Introduction. In A. Hickey-Moody & P. Malins (Eds.), *Deleuzian encounters: Studies in contemporary social issues* (pp. 1–24). London: Palgrave.

Ihonen, M. (1999). *Naisen paikka lestadiolaisuudessa. Varhaisia juonteita.* Esitelmä Turussa 15.10.1999 [Presentation paper: "Woman in the seventeenth century Laestadianism. The early trails"]. Retrieved from http://people.uta.fi/~tlmaih/Jutut2/naiskuva.htm

Ihonen, M. (2001). *Vaikenevat naiset. Keskustelua naisen paikasta 1800-luvun lestadiolaisuudessa* [The silent women. Discussion on the place of a woman in 19th-century Laestadianism]. *Historiallinen Aikakauskirja, 99*(3), 276–292.

Irigaray, L. (1993). *Je, tu, nous.* New York: Routledge.

Kutuniva, M. (2007). Keskusteluja naiseudesta, vanhoillislestadiolaisesta uskosta ja uskonnosta [Discussions on womanhood, Conservative Laestadian faith and religion]. In M. Autti, S. Keskitalo-Foley, P. Naskali, & H. Sinevaara-Niskanen (Eds.), *Kuulumisia—feministisiä tulkintoja naisten toimijuuksista* [Feminist interpretations on women's agencies]. (pp. 17–36). Rovaniemi: Lapland University Press.

Leivo, S. (2001). Jeesuksen nimessä ja veressä. Synninpäästön käyttöönotosta lestadiolaisuudessa. In J. Talonen & I. Harjutsalo (Eds.), *Lestadiolaisuuden monet kasvot* [The many faces of Laestadianism]. (pp. 103–121). *Iustitia 14* Suomen Teologisen Instituutin Aikakauskirja.

Mahmood, S. (2012). *The politics of piety. The Islamic revival and the feminist subject.* Princeton, NJ: Princeton University Press.

Malins, P. (2007). City folds: Injecting drug use and urban space. In A. Hickey-Moody & P. Malins (Eds.), *Deleuzian encounters: Studies in contemporary social issues* (pp. 151–168). London: Palgrave.

Manning, E. (2013). *Always more than one.* Durham, NC: Duke University Press.

Massumi, B. (2002). *Parables for the virtual.* Durham, NC: Duke University Press.

Nancy, J.L. (2000). *Being singular plural.* Stanford, CA: Stanford University Press.

Smith, D.W. (2001). The doctrine of univocity: Deleuze's ontology of immanence. In M. Bryden (Ed.), *Deleuze and religion* (pp. 167–183). London: Routledge.

Stagoll, C. (2010). Becoming. In A. Parr (Ed.), *The Deleuze dictionary* (pp. 25–27). New York: Columbia University Press.

Whitehead, A.N. (1978/1985). *Process and reality* (Corrected ed). D.R. Griffin & D.W. Sherburne (Eds.). New York: The Free Press.

SECTION THREE:
FINAL THOUGHTS ON
CRITICAL RESEARCH IN MOTION

[W]riting ... can be affirmative and inventive. Invention requires experimentation ... The first rule of thumb if you want to invent or reinvent concepts is simple: don't apply them ... One device for avoiding application is to adopt an "exemplary method." ... An example is neither general (as is a system of concepts) nor particular (as is the material to which a system is applied). It is "singular." (Massumi, 2002, p. 17)

FLUIDITY HERE IS the uncertain and still infinite instability of the movement, which is also the open-ended and experimental force in methodology, making analysis with desire possible and explicit. In its openness, it works well within temporal, but situated, explorations in the realms of critical social research. The critical situated exploration *is* the "exemplary method" in itself as it includes the potentials (processes and techniques) of inquiry within which to study them. As life is the focus of the inquiry it only needs methodologies, concepts, theories, and methods to exemplify and activate the details of the studied processes.

This is to follow the inspirations of the inquiry, the data production, the data, and its analysis stimulated by scientific concepts and the intensities they bring—for instance, the reading of women's aspirations inspired to connect them with desire into desiring machines. The methodologies used activate the studied material with their movement, but the material also sets these scientific systems, concepts, ideas, and modules into motion and creates always its own situated firsthand "exemplary methods." These different re-creations can be novel in their composition, but they are never original, since they emerge from the midst of a methodological ocean of multiple perspectives, practices, and failed experimentations. (See Deleuze, 1994; M. Koro-Ljungberg, personal communication, November 2, 2018.)

The last section of the book discusses the possibilities of fluid methodologies and their contribution for the future of feminist critical social qualitative inquiry. The purpose is also to discuss the multitude of challenges that these involve. At the end of the section, the possible futures of fluid methodologies are discussed with Professor Mirka Koro-Ljungberg.

CHAPTER SIX

The Possibilities and Challenges of the Methodologies in Motion

IN STUDYING SOCIAL issues within feminist methodology, the emphasis is on the subtleness and openness of the inquiry to learn ways of knowing differently. In this process of inquiry, the fluid processes of life, expressions, articulations, intensities, and affects are influenced by methods and theories and become data, which require employing experimental tools to examine their movement. This involves an experimentalist take on the inquiry through acceptance of the uncertainty of the infiniteness of the inquiry and in forming an approach to create more adaptable ways of doing qualitative research in order to understand complex social issues. Experimentation is a processual practice, which does not seize the processes under study, but instead continues producing more data through the examination. Therefore, the experimental approach concerns and involves the entire process of inquiry, its data production, and analysis, which always ends up producing something differently.

Within poststructuralist methodology, the collective data production is not simply a question of conducting a study together with the participants but about keeping the process of inquiry open for the unexpected and exploring our ways of being and knowing together. To produce data together means taking the risk of not knowing, and continuing without knowing what would follow, what is produced, with what outcomes and effects, and for whom. Here, to experiment is the reason why something is studied: to be able to produce a shift in methodological thinking. Here, this shift in methodology becomes crucial because it allows for a focus on the production of difference and to examine it beyond comparison and judgment.

The experimental approach, within collective data production, enables openness and infiniteness, which bear the potential to affect and be affected. This is important in examining social issues and their temporary constellations, as data productions have to be open for various readings and understandings to have significance beyond their situated processes of inquiry. The infiniteness also stresses openness "to the new" (Grosz, 1999), which signifies the non-linear motion in methodology intersecting the future with present and past. This enables the inquiry to be perceived as a constantly evolving constellation in which novel conceptualizations, approaches, techniques, and understandings take place. This shifts critical social research toward an inquiry that moves in, between, and beyond normative and often victimizing constructions.

Since the poststructuralist analysis works within open-ended data, it goes beyond the expected in examining processes in which we aspire and are constantly and differently constituted (see Lather, 2007). This allows the researcher not to follow any pre-given instructions or models, but instead requires letting data and events take the lead in the inquiry. The focus was therefore on occupying a plot, in other words, capturing the event and examining the movements, changes, and ruptures in it. As previously discussed, this required changing the focus from the women's voices to the encounters and processes in which these were expressed. Therefore, my thinking occurred not through the interpretations of the data but through the lines the women's aspirations produced and the flows, arrests, and ruptures of the lines occurring in the data. These ruptures opened possibilities for viewing the data through the events in which the data did not flow, produced silences, or took new routes.

Reading the data with desire is to understand desire in contrast to the common way of understanding it as a subject's choice and a self-explanatory movement of reflection, as "I did this, and I reflect on it" (Holland, 2013, pp. 33–34); instead, this reading enables one to understand desire as an open force that varies in the hands of analysts during the process of inquiry (Deleuze & Guattari, 1987). The concept of desire was needed to reach beyond the commonsense view of the human as the centralized power agent reflecting on the world and to challenge the mediated image of reflection that as a system is incapable of challenging or transforming the established order of things (see Deleuze & Guattari, 1983, 1994; Deleuze, 1994; MacMahon, 2005). As desire operates within temporal arrangements (Deleuze & Guattari, 1983), they cannot be taken to represent the person's reality, as for instance, the striated lines of Laestadian women's faith do not constitute their experience and reality as strictly following the teachings of a religious movement but only indicate the different temporary formations their lines make. Desire as a force has no subject or object; it lies not in the unconsciousness, as there is no unconsciousness. It has to be manufactured (Deleuze & Guattari, 1983). However, it manages to provide the needed multi-layered processuality in the examination of difference and minority beyond preordained positions and identifications.

6.1. THE AFTERMATHS OF FLUID FEMINIST CRITICAL SOCIAL INQUIRY

Feminist poststructuralist methods are often used in examining difference and subjects considered oppressed, victimized, or lacking agency—topics which, in their sensitiveness, involve particularly subtle methods of inquiry. These topics often involve understanding difference as differences within (see Mohanty, 1984; Spivak, 1997, 1999; Braidotti, 2008; Keskinen, 2012). Understanding differences within allows also an understanding of methodologies being at the same time relational and open-ended, as all the processes from research interests and data production to analysis are intertwined and nonlinear. As they overlap, they are part of producing one another; the analysis is part of the data production as the analysis incites further research interests, as happens often in the process of the inquiry.

Fluidity in research suggests that methods are understood as evolvements of changing and slippery data, a thought that questions the possibility of ready-made methods and techniques of inquiry (see Koro-Ljungberg & MacLure, 2013a), and data are continuously produced in open-ended processes of inquiry as data are everything we produce through scientific examination (see Koro-Ljungberg, 2013, 2016; Koro-Ljungberg, Carlson, Tesar, & Anderson, 2015; see also Taylor et al., 2019). Also, these fluid methodologies understand data as something that form themselves in connections and productions with other data. This means that there are no data that would be separate from the processes of their production. The production of data therefore *is* the data (Koro-Ljungberg, 2013, 2016; Koro-Ljungberg & MacLure, 2013a; Koro-Ljungberg, Carlson, Tesar & Anderson, 2015). This processuality of changing and uneven data production enables a shift toward more ethical and processual ways of inquiry. It requires understanding the subject of the study and its processes more broadly, since the data production processes are not singular and separate, but shared collaborative productions that evolve even while being studied.

Following this line of thinking, methods are produced and producing, generating data in the process of a study as much as data produce and fabricate methods. Thus, similarly, for instance, the method of collaborative writing is created in (the mappings of) the storylines, comments, notes, and responses.

Thus, perceiving data as generative means that it could not be studied separately outside its processes. This also allows avoiding positioning the participants and examining, for instance, their voice and agency as such. The interest in this fluid methodology is not therefore to construct a narrative of an individual subject; rather, it is to examine the multiple and shifting processes in which these formations are produced. However, this is not to suggest that these processes were not situated. On the contrary. Situating the temporary negotiations and constellations of subjectivity brings them into existence. The focus on process allows avoiding limiting and stopping the movement in the studied data, since constellations such as subject and identity are considered to be only the by-products of these continuous negotiations. Even if these constellations are present in the form of intensities or affects (in the modalities of subjectivity: expressions and enunciations) in the data production, they do not always matter; in other words, they become explicit in the descriptions of the events and encounters.

However, these multiple (re)constructions or creations of the data also seem ontologically connected to understanding the research as an experiment. This is a significant move from systemic collective production into more creative ways of working within the accidental and the unexpected in data production. At the same time, within the data production, the focus of the study shifts from examining voiced experience to examining the processes in which the experiences form intensities and movement in the data. The interest is now on the processes, which produce data in intra-action with the other immediate productions and processes. In these processes, the concern is no longer about the authenticity of the data, or in focusing on the actual voices of the participants nor on thinking of the validity and evidence of the study (Lather, 1997, 2007). Rather, it is about an open-ended approach affording an understanding of the various productions, such as enunciations, texts, and analyses, all to be part of the data production, since these are involved in generating the data.

This approach to data production means doing research differently, working without a clear plan and an idea of how to proceed. This way of working does not necessarily aim to produce knowledge that is traditionally considered scientifically valid since its significance is in the generative but leaking processes that are not necessarily quantifiable, easily classified, or labeled due to their messiness and entangledness. However, with the focus on the methods in-the-making this data production manages to question the normativity of the already set practices of traditional data production and the knowledge it can create (Lather, 2007, 2016; St. Pierre, 2013). This is not to oppose other ways of data production, but to offer an alternative way to create data in which the creations are in-the-making together with its human, social, and non-human elements in the encounters. Working with this living data raises questions of what data can do and how these productions ethically matter (see Koro-Ljungberg & MacLure, 2013a; Barad, 2003, 2007), and what the effects are of the data production, whom or what does this work for, and for what kind of purposes (Foucault, 1983).

In critical social inquiries, the participants are often seen positioned in a discourse with built-in expectations concerning their minority status and the need for voice and agency. However, often the purpose is not to position the participants in victimizing discourses but to enable them to operate outside these. To avoid fixed positions, positions that reinforce the "normal," is to create practices of inquiry and analysis that go beyond normative discourses (Braidotti & Pisters, 2012). This often requires producing data with participants and the use of processual, collective, and open-ended methods of inquiry to produce data differently within and beyond these discourses.

Employing collective open-ended methods offers a space for collaborative productions to evolve beyond victimized positions and the need to judge and categorize. The focus on processes brings them forth and to be seen, felt and lived, in other words, to matter (Deleuze, 1998). To be able to recognize differences without judgment and comparison requires moving away from examining the victimized individuals or the victimizing structures, but to focus on their processes to examine them beyond the humanist narratives and experiences. Hence, there is no need to speak for them or on behalf of them, but to go beyond this binary thinking of us and them, me, and others altogether (see Alcoff, 2009; Chaudhry, 2009). Since the data are collectively produced but affectively lived, it enables examination of enunciations, articulations, and (bodily) expressions, making them neither collective nor individual.

However, the focus being on processes could be a challenge in claiming research validity, since, to produce validity in research in the traditional sense, one must produce something of the same within the present criteria, something that would be understandable within predominant scientific discourses (Koro-Ljungberg, 2016). Instead, here, the processuality challenges the traditional authorized and legitimized research by following unorthodox methods and by producing fluid and changing data. This challenges overly static and universalized Western humanist inquiry, which by producing unified knowledge subjugates all other ways of knowing (Spivak, 1988). To challenge this univocality requires experimenting with the open-ended processes that allow change, and complex and multiple outcomes, which thus contributes by understanding difference not as the opposite of the same, but as an essential part of (un)producing the same. This does not mean eliminating the difference between ourselves and those we study as an attempt to relate to represent them (MacLure, 2013b). Rather, in order to understand difference, it needs to be problematized. For instance, accepting the difference, the diversity, partiality, and changing nature of the data and inquiry, and the incompleteness of the truth and knowledge they produce, helps to overcome the need to think through categories and binaries.

Also, the collective production of data disturbs the binary of me and the other and promotes the unwillingness to position the collaborators with the emancipatory actions that othering often entails. The emancipatory politics can be considered a part of the metanarrative of liberation of humankind in which the so-called other is understood to grant power from the privileged researcher (see, e.g., Humphries, 2000). The debates on otherness and insider-outsider perspectives are made redundant by the poststructuralist understanding of experience as continuously co-produced (see Deleuze, 1994, 1991). Since experience is constantly being produced, it is also part of life's immanent productions, making it fluid and capable of overcoming the binary of the researcher and the researched. Therefore, the situated but equally multifaceted and diverse negotiations actively shape the prevailing and normative societal discourses concerning difference and agency in minority (Deleuze, 2006; Haraway, 1988; see also Haraway, 2004).

6.2 SOME FUTURE POSSIBILITIES AND CHALLENGES OF FLUID METHODOLOGIES IN CRITICAL SOCIAL RESEARCH

Fluidity and movement in methodology can be challenging to think about and work with, especially for beginning researchers, because as well as the inquiry, the methodology changes during the process and depending on the studied event. However, fluidity and movement offer space for creativity and flexibility to think with theories, methods, and techniques of inquiry, and assist in approaching oppressive social and political situations and challenging issues with subtlety. Since these fluid and experimental methodologies are challenging to grasp, they were discussed with Professor Mirka Koro-Ljungberg, who has both taught and written extensively on postmethodology and on the use of experimental methods. Our conversation concerned fluidity in critical qualitative research and what kind of ethical questions it brings into today's practices of inquiry and the effects it has on the future of the study of feminist and social justice issues within qualitative research. The symbol ⏵ within the discussion expresses the pauses, the movement of thinking, breathing, non-verbal expressions in speech cut from the transcriptions. We began with the question of how to think of fluidity in critical social qualitative research:

> Mirka: Fluidity is ⏵ sensitivity to the fact that things are more in flux. When I talk about fluidity it is not this circular notion that qualitative researchers have talked a long time about. The design goes in cycles and you need to revisit the questions because that is still based on ⏵ modifying what I have already created.

> Mirka: The question is not what it is; it is what fluidity does, and once we move from the definition to the function ⏵ it is easier to understand that fluidity is not a singular definition, some sort of predictable entity but ⏵ it works as a shifty methodological space ⏵ I am now talking about ⏵ methodology, carrying out an inquiry or implementing or thinking about inquiry. What becomes challenging is the planning and deciding if you think that the planning and deciding means that you are able as a researcher to somehow predict your tools or predict the knowledge that is being produced ⏵

Teija: [Is] that fluidity a space —

Mirka: It is a move from fixed, stable, objective notions of methodology and methods to more emergent. I am using Deleuze['s] "becoming space" where things can come together, or they might not come together in sometimes unexpected and sometimes even expected ways that the whole process of becoming or relating is unpredictable.

Teija: Does it mean that you have to move from one space to another?

Mirka: If you think critical work including feminis[t], critical theories, post-theories so in a way you don't need to do this transformation [move from one space to another] if you open up the concept of critical [to include the various critical approaches]. If you want to stick with the more narrow notion of criticality that there are some kind of posts of oppression — and of inequity that are fixed I think that the fluid methodologies could work around those posts; so, let's say that gender post is fixed — the — methodological components — the conceptual or the theoretical — are still creating constellation[s] around [it] — so for me, it doesn't have to be either [or].

Teija: What does — fluidity bring to the critical [methodologies]?

Mirka: I started to talk about the fluid methodological spaces — because I — observed that regardless of your theoretical orientation whether you are positivist, phenomenologist, critical theorist, poststructuralist you have — ideologies that are shifting; like let's think about Butler's performativity. The gender is performed, is not — fixed — it is situated — but the methodologies are fixed — so this was the kind of call to create more sensitivity to the fact that if your — ideologies are built on situated knowledges [referring to Donna Haraway's (1988) notion concerning the nature of knowledge not as objective but as situational] therefore your methods should also do that, then the idea that [for] poststructuralism, postmodernism and posts it is easier because the flux is *it*, everything is in flux. But in the critical work, if we do more traditional work it becomes challenging because there are some things that are not in flux and those are usually the elements that [have] to do with inequity, e.g., race, poverty —

Mirka: My proposition is that you could think about for example a pool, a whirlpool, everything is shifting and moving and all the floating elements are coming together in some ways but there are some posts in the pool that are holding the net — of the waterball so that the system is still in flux, even though it has couple of stable elements that are fixed in real. Therefore, I see that fluidity could also work for critical people who are not willing to completely 100 percent buy into situated knowledges and fluidity because of that inequity, oppression.

Teija: Exactly! So how does the fluidity and the kind of flow of the water affect now the posts in the water? — what does it do [to] the situatedness [of the poles] and the ethics?

Mirka: — Let's not go to the ethic[s] question yet, because what you are raising here is what happens to the posts in the floating water. And I think that if you think about the posts being iron or some sort of metal, for example, drawing from physics or sort of, so what happens when the water interacts with the post? There is continuous, or almost like a surfacing effect even though there is this solid post in the flowing water, it is continuously being, it continuously interacts with the water, sometimes even creating a corroding effect, so the post could actually corrode to the point that it is being dissolved.

Mirka: So, I think that that is kind of a really interesting space of change and transformation, because it could be really slow, think about, for example, let's do a — female post, the notion of oppressed woman, or — what feminists would kind of, you know, kind of hold on some way. But because the water is continuously flowing and moving and bringing objects to be in touch, to have a contact with that post, the post is ultimately changing — and sometimes even the deeper structures are being affected because they are part of the ecological system, e.g., the water. So, I think feminists would also say that the role of the "woman" — has not been the same for hundreds of years, so it is changing in the socio-political context, the socio-political water as the pressure is changing even if the post would be a post of the oppression of the female gender. It is changing because it is part of the system. Or kind of systems thinking or kind of ecological approach to methodology, it would help to see that even though we have a post, we have these floating things, the post is some ways also changing even though it could be a long time before it gets corroded — or but there is that corrosion — but there is that exposure that creates some sort of transformation, even in the molecular, or minor scale or more major scale depending what happens.

Teija: So, it is active, so fluidity is in a way — for me it is a kind of, well, moving, changing, and affective force.

Teija: — could say that fluidity and movement — are — basic forces

Mirka: About space — I didn't think that is like a void space but it is an active space that has also forces and energy in it, otherwise the particles wouldn't be moving, so I think — about movement and fluidity as a force-feel, or even as a force, an active force —

Teija: [In using fluid methodologies] we cannot predict the ethics and what [they will] bring because we don't know the situations — and what [will] happen — we can only experiment —

Mirka: Ethics can no longer be a duty or a compliance because — the whole notion of — predictable ethical conduct becomes a problem. Here I am drawing from Derrida, and the notion of responsibility — the ultimate ethical question is being responsive to the difference — Derrida talks about meeting the other — [while being] — willing, ready to meet the other — in this case could be methodological, theoretical — ontological difference but something that is or differs from me, differs from my world, my expectations how things are going to go — to practice that is really hard —

Teija: That is — maybe the same what Deleuze, Braidotti, and others talk about. Some kind of sustainable ethics in a way that you have — compassion and [think of] the consequences which [the inquiry] produce[s].

Teija: — what the movement in methodology could give to the future [of critical social inquiry]? How would fluid methodologies assist in understanding the different ontologies, realities, we have in the world?

Mirka: Some of the challenges for beginning researchers would be to be comfortable in the fluid methodological space — I feel there is so much to take in, in terms of language and the techniques — that people just get overwhelmingly lost, not productively lost but lost so deeply that they can no longer engage in the inquiry if I drop them in the fluid spaces, so the challenge is that you need to have enough knowledge, methodological knowledge, and theoretical and conceptual knowledge plus an attitude, a willingness to be able to carry out your inquiry in these unpredictable shifting spaces.

Mirka: — it is completely fine to say that I am not fine with that kind of unpredictability but — that type of flexibility or continuous change — fuels the inquiry and makes us more curious of what is going to happen, how we are going to change, the world is going to change as a result of these shifts and transformations.

Mirka: So then, what could this kind of inquiry offer? I think that goes back to that how I got into this was the problem with the fixed methods and the idea that the methods, also methodologies and techniques, are not responding to the shifting cultural and political contexts — we can do only so much in terms of changing — or transforming practices with the methods that are fixed, kind of ancient and old and — would not match the societal, cultural, and political climate.

Mirka: So fluid methodological spaces and fluidity as a force enable us to think — the socio-political context, where we carry out our research and live with the methods, and the types of tools and techniques that we use to inquire on, [as a] shifting target — I think that type of alignment with techniques, ideology, and existing context is one big possibility of fluid methodologies — and also the idea that there are shifts and currents in the socio-cultural-political lives of ours that then could — be affecting the techniques and approaches we are using — compared to the system where everything is grounded, predictable and somehow needs to be validated and verified with some sort of historical knowledge before it can be implemented —

Mirka: Creating something emerging and responsive [to the context] is almost unethical to these kinds of discourses because the validity [in them] is based on repeated measures etc. These kinds of systems of inquiry, methodological systems, are less capable of adapting to the kind of changes that are coming from the field or the lives that our participants encounter. [This] is the lack that the fixed methodologies always experience ⸺ [and which] fluidity ⸺ could [reduce].

Teija: ⸺ When you use them [fluid methodologies] you realize that you cannot really have a method, a system because you don't want to fix things ⸺

Mirka: But ⸺ it doesn't mean ⸺ unpreparedness. It is ⸺ kind of carrying the potential with you, [to] think that I didn't have a method, but I had all the methods.

Teija: ⸺ You try to keep an open mind ⸺ to serve the particular needs of the inquiry.

Mirka: ⸺ Rather than planning to predict or planning to implement a particular technique or a method now you carry with you the possibility of any method, all methods. So, I think what it changes is the way that you implement, choose or adapt or modify techniques. It does not start from you but the first stimulus comes from elsewhere so that ⸺ the interaction is initiated from not your predictable ⸺ methodological mind, it is elsewhere within the ecology.

Teija: The stimuli are ⸺ beyond our ⸺

Mirka: Almost like the call ⸺ for interaction. Something that ⸺ is not researcher-driven. What a researcher could do is [to be] available ⸺ until [s/he] encounter[s] something, or something encounters [her/him].

As understood, to work within fluid methodologies, or methodological spaces goes beyond attempts to examine something in order to know it and to define it, such as difference, gender, race, but it is "an exploration [...] toward movement, toward a relational stance that makes it impossible to pin down knowledge but asks us instead to invent" (Manning, 2007, p. xvi). Manning offers an alternative, a politics of touch, of sensing to be able to work also outside the linear timeline, in space-time, enabling to authorize situated knowledges emerging in the transculturation-in-movement and to "inquire into democracies-to-come and to wonder what politics might become were we capable of reinventing it" (p. xvi). Similarly, within critical social inquiries this is to engage to the lines of difference and marginality, in which the expressions, articulations, intensities, bodies, and affects become acted upon. For a researcher, to be able to engage to the lines coming from studied everyday ecologies requires making oneself available for the interactions and encounters they request. This, within the ethics of feminist methodology, means staying with the trouble, remaining close to the intensities, affects, and politics of life, while seeking to become kin with the world to make more liveable and connected futures (Haraway, 2016). In fluid feminist methodology and critical social inquiry this means constantly residing with emergent movement and its potencies in an inquiry and in its processes to enable being, becoming, and knowing differently:

> In reality, life is a movement, materiality is the inverse movement, and each of these two movements is simple, the matter which forms a world being an undivided flux, and undivided also the life that runs through it, cutting out in it living beings all along its track. (Bergson, 1911, p. 249)

References

Data
Personal communication with Professor Mirka Koro-Ljungberg, 2 November 2018.

Literature
Alcoff, L. (2009). The problem of speaking for others. In A.Y. Jackson & L. Mazzei (Eds.), *Voice in qualitative inquiry: Challenging conventional, interpretive, and critical conceptions in qualitative research* (pp. 116–135). London and New York: Routledge.

Barad, K. (2003). Posthumanist performativity: Toward an understanding of how matter comes to matter. *Signs: Journal of Women in Culture and Society, 28*(3), 801–831.

Barad, K. (2007). *Meeting the universe halfway: Quantum physics and the entanglement of matter and meaning*. Durham, NC: Duke University Press.

Bergson, H. (1911). *Creative evolution*. A. Mitchell (Trans.). New York: Henry Holt. Retrieved from https://www.gutenberg.org/files/26163/26163-h/26163-h.htm

Braidotti, R. (2008). In spite of the times. The postsecular turn in feminism. *Theory, Culture & Society, 25*(6), 1–24.

Braidotti, R., & Pisters, P. (2012). Introduction. In R. Braidotti & P. Pisters (Eds.), *Revisiting normativity with Deleuze* (pp. 1–8). London: Bloomsbury.

Chaudhry, L.N. (2009). Forays into the mist: Violences, voices, and vignettes. In A.Y. Jackson & L. Mazzei (Eds.), *Voice in qualitative inquiry. Challenging conventional, interpretive, and critical conceptions in qualitative research* (pp. 137–163). London and New York: Routledge.

Deleuze, G. (1991). *Empiricism and subjectivity: An essay on Hume's theory of human nature*. (C.V. Boundas, Trans.). New York: Columbia University Press.

Deleuze, G. (1994). *Difference and repetition*. (P. Patton, Trans.). New York: Columbia University Press.

Deleuze, G. (1998). *Essays critical and clinical*. (D.W. Smith & M.A. Greco, Trans.). Burchill, London, UK: Verso.

Deleuze, G. (2006). *Foucault*. (S. Hand, Ed. and Trans.). London: Continuum.

Deleuze, G., & Guattari, F. (1983). *Anti-Oedipus: Capitalism and schizophrenia*. (R. Hurley, M. Seem, & H.R. Lane, Trans). London: Athlone.

Deleuze, G., & Guattari, F. (1987). *A thousand plateaus: Capitalism and schizophrenia*. (B. Massumi, Trans.). Minneapolis: University of Minnesota Press.

Deleuze, G., & Guattari, F. (1994). *What is philosophy?* (H. Tomlinson & G. Burchell, Trans.). New York: Columbia University Press.

Foucault, M. (1983). Forewords. In G. Deleuze & F. Guattari, *Anti-Oedipus: Capitalism and schizophrenia*. (R. Hurley, M. Seem & H.R. Lane, Trans.) (pp. xi–xiv). London: Athlone.

Grosz, E. (1999). Becoming... An introduction. In E. Grosz (Ed.), *Explorations in time, memory and futures* (pp. 1–12). Ithaca, NY, and London: Cornell University Press.

Grosz, E. (1999). Thinking the New: Of Futures yet unthought. In E. Grosz (Ed.), *Explorations in time, memory and futures* (pp.15–28). Ithaca and London: Cornell University Press.

Haraway, D.J. (1988). Situated knowledges: The science question in feminism and the privilege of partial perspective. *Feminist Studies (14)*, 575–599.

Haraway, D.J. (2004). The promises of monsters: A generative politics for inappropriate/d others. In D.J. Haraway (Ed.), *The Haraway reader* (pp. 63–124). London: Routledge.

Haraway, D.J. (2015). *Reconceptualizing qualitative research: Methodologies without methodology.* Thousand Oaks, CA: Sage.

Haraway, D.J. (2016). *Staying with the trouble. Making kin in the Chthulucene.* Durham, NC, and London: Duke University Press.

Holland, E.W. (2013). *Deleuze and Guattari's A Thousand Plateaus.* London: Bloomsbury.

Humphries, B. (2000). From critical theory to emancipatory action: Contradictory research goals? In C. Truman & B. Humphries (Eds.), *Research and inequality* (pp. 179-190). London: UCL Press.

Keskinen, S. (2012). Kulttuurilla merkityt toiset ja universaalin käsittelyn paradoksi väkivaltatyössä. [Culturally labelled others and the paradox of universality in violence prevention work]. In S. Keskinen, J. Vuori & A. Hirsiaho (Eds.), *Monikulttuurisuuden sukupuoli. Kansalaisuus ja erot hyvinvointiyhteiskunnassa* [Gendered multiculturalism. Citizenship and difference in the welfare society] (pp. 291–320). Tampere, Finland: Tampere University Press.

Koro-Ljungberg, M. (2013). "Data" as vital illusion. *Cultural Studies <=> Critical Methodologies, 13*(4), 274–278.

Koro-Ljungberg, M., & MacLure, M. (2013). Provocations, re-un-visions, death, and other possibilities of "data." *Cultural Studies <=> Critical Methodologies, 13*(4), 219–222.

Koro-Ljungberg, M., Carlson, D., Tesar, M., & Anderson, K. (2015). Methodology brut: Philosophy, ecstatic thinking, and some other (unfinished) things. *Qualitative Inquiry, 21*(7), 612–619.

Koro-Ljungberg, M. (2016). *Reconceptualizing qualitative research. Methodologies without methodology.* Thousand Oaks, CA: Sage.

Lather, P. (1997). Drawing the line at Angels: Working the ruins of feminist ethnography. *Qualitative Studies in Education, 10*(3), 285–304.

Lather, P. (2007). *Getting lost: Feminist efforts towards a double(d) science.* Albany: State University of New York Press.

Lather, P. (2016). Killing the mother? Butler after Barad in feminist (post)qualitative research. In A.B. Reinertsen (Ed.), *Becoming Earth: A posthuman turn in* educational discourse. *Collapsing Nature/Culture Divides* (pp. 21–30). Rotterdam: Sense Publishing.

MacLure, M. (2013a). The wonder of data. *Cultural Studies <=> Critical Methodologies, 13*(4), 228–232.

MacLure, M. (2013b). Classification or wonder? Coding as an Analytic Practice in Qualitative Research. In J. Ringrose & R. Coleman (Eds.), *Deleuze and research methodologies* (pp. 164–183). Edinburgh University Press.

MacMahon, M. (2005). Difference and repetition. In C. Stivale (Ed.), *Gilles Deleuze: Key concepts* (pp. 42–52). Chesham, UK: Acumen.

Manning, E. (2007). *Politics of touch. Sense, movement, sovereignty.* Minneapolis and London: University of Minnesota Press.

Massumi, B. (2002). *Parables for the virtual.* Durham, NC: Duke University Press.

Mohanty, C.T. (1984). Under Western eyes: Feminist scholarship and colonial discourses. *Boundary 2. (12)*3, 333–358. Retrieved from http://www2.kobe-u.ac.jp/~alexroni/IPD%202015%20readings/IPD%202015_5/under-western-eyes.pdf

Spivak, G. (1988). Can the subaltern speak? In C. Nelson & L. Grossberg (Eds.), *Marxism and the interpretation of culture* (pp. 271–313). London: Macmillan.

Spivak, G. (1997). In a word: Interview. In L. Nicholson (Ed.), *The second wave: A reader in feminist theory* (pp. 356–378). New York: Routledge.

Spivak, G. (1999). *A critique of postcolonial reason. Toward a history of vanishing present.* Cambridge, MA: Harvard University Press.

St. Pierre, E.A. (2013). The posts continue: Becoming. *International Journal of Qualitative Studies in Education, 26*(6), 646–657.

Taylor, C., Fairchild, N., Koro-Ljungberg, M., Carey, N., Benozzo, A., & Elmenhorst, C. (2019). Improvising bags choreographies: Disturbing normative ways of doing research. *Qualitative Inquiry, 25*(1), 17–25.

Glossary

Affect enfolds in every human and non-human encounter and event, taking different forms from atmospheres, feelings, and reactions to embodied and produced intensities and sensations as the affect exceeds singular and bounded human bodies and existence.

Aspirations are understood here as changing coded constellations fueled by desire.

Becoming is the transformational and the unexpected element in the production of subjectivity. Becoming consists of continuous processes of subtle differenciation due to the current conditions allowing one to create and to be created within many changing dispositions. Becoming is always relational and therefore it cannot be removed from its milieu and contexts, its arrangement.

Becoming-woman is a process which works toward unfolding from the various constraints of the social world. Becoming-woman also works as a threshold to a minority becoming. It is an ethical and critical process of claiming the position of marginal (not in a humanist, but in a posthumanist sense) understanding of the human as part of ecologies of the world. Because becoming-woman is the passage to all the ways to exist, since womanhood is a cultural landmark of inequality and oppression, this becoming requires the location of the decentered to enable its transformation.

Collective refers to the connected lines of various enunciations, expressions, and articulations.

Decentered becoming is the experience of a minority, of difference, which is required to be able to transform the knowledge in positions of power. Minority becoming is to transform, to become imperceptible, to avoid taking established forms such as the subject with fixed identities and genealogies, but instead to take the various locations, which the transformational process has to offer, as the starting point for thinking and acting.

Desire is understood here as the fundamental productive force 'fueling' the production of connections, becoming, and necessary differences. Desire is a force without inbuilt intentionality against its common interpretation as a lack or as sexual desire oriented toward objects and fulfillment.

Desiring machines are the arrangements of desire that produce lines and function within schizoanalysis.

Differenciation is a force dispersed in all becoming material or non-material existence. See also *becoming*.

Dispositions are arrangements of desire, being produced as a side product of desire in the everyday living. They are about establishing one's technique of balancing movement, rest, speed, and slowness in one's lines.

Immanent. Transcendent. Transcendental. Immanent reality is about connecting and becoming, which is possible without the abstract and transcendent outside for humans to reflect on. It is the "real," which is not mediated, but it is not subjected either. Immanent works with transcendental, as it is the force of actualizing within produced social and religious realities. Transcendent denotes values and attributes which are not immanent and become possible only through production with immanent flows of desire. The immanent flows cannot be produced. The difference between transcendent and transcendental forces is that the former stands as the opposite to immanent forces whereas the latter is the force operating together with the immanent in the process of actualization.

Lines. The desiring machines produce forces, which are depicted here as lines. These lines intersect and form the multidimensional layers of social currents, flows, and connections which are mapped to enable their examination. These lines can gather together and are also able to form arrangements, like groups, actions, enactments, and structures, packed with forces.

Machinic comprises the connections and flows necessary to express the actual in desire, which makes these passions and intensities to matter. This force is found in resonances and vibrations as it functions through connections.

Modalities. Modalities refer here to the certain constitutive elements of subjectivity processes, understood as enunciations, articulations, and arrangements of expressions as well as embodied actions, affects, and practices.

Molar. Molecular. Religion is produced here by, for instance, molar structural lines of congregations and through more disparate molecular faith. Consequently, religion could be interpreted through its molar constructions of spiritual power and political domination, but also through productive desire connecting it to molecular lines producing it as faith. However, there are no molar aggregates of productions without the singularly differentiated lines. In contrast to the religious collective productions, which are external and governing, the singular lines *are* the productions. Nevertheless, even these singular lines connected to machinic religious desiring machines manage to produce molecular packs, but also collectives.

Schizoanalysis is the experimental approach of Gilles Deleuze and Félix Guattari used to examine the changing formations of subjectivity through multi-layered analysis. For analysis, this multi-layeredness means combining various social, personal, and affective layers of processes of subjectivity formation for simultaneous examination.

Glossary

Secular becoming-woman is, for religious women, the state of claiming identity and subjectivity. This minority becoming functions as the threshold, intermediate space in which to operate with different identities and nomadic ways of being. The state of mapping the coordinates of one's becoming.

Subjectivity is a process that enables one to become temporarily a subject. This becoming is possible through events, changes, and breaks in the collective productions, through which one articulates, negotiates, and forms temporary modalities, arrangements of subjectivity. This way these arrangements do not make subjects as such but subjectivities, processes of formation always situated by the current conditions.

Author Bio

Dr. Teija Rantala received her Master's in Education and her doctorate in Gender Studies from the University of Helsinki. In her doctoral dissertation, she studied women belonging to religious revival movement in Finland. She employed experimental methodology and created analyses to examine the women's desires on their maternal and female subjectivity and the changes and differences in these processes. Teija has lectured on the ethics and methods of her research at several universities (e.g., University of Helsinki, Finland; University of Ghent, Belgium; and University of Aberystwyth, Wales, UK). She has also published numerous open access journal articles and co-edited the publication *Darkness Matters* for RERM. Currently, her interests are in examining how, in collective data production, the idea of time and temporality is constituted.

Index

A

affect, xiii–xvi, 4, 5, 41, 53, 56, 57, 58, 71, 72, 73, 80, 81, 84, 86, 95, 98, 107
   in feminist methodology, 19–20
   and memory, Spinozian, 25
   and writing, 27, 42
affective
   intensities, 3, 43, 56
   processes, 5, 7, 48, 112
   conditions, 9
   nature, 15
   ways of expression, 22
   vision, 25
   memories, 42
   materialities, 53
   events, 56
   movement, 59
   states, 88
   force, 104
   affectively lived, 23, 100
   affectively connected, 83
arrangement, 57, 60, 66, 71, 72, 74, 75, 79, 81, 84, 86, 112
   of memory, 25
   of force-feel, 59
   of desire, 59–60, 61, 63, 65, 87, 96, 112
   of abstract machines, 62
   machinic, 62, 78
   living, of forces, 78
   structured, molar, molecular, 86
   becoming and, 111
   of subjectivity, 113
   Also see desiring machines; see lines
articulation, 12, 15, 24, 25, 41, 42, 57–59, 62, 71, 72, 73, 75, 95, 100, 107
   collective, 111
aspiration, 37, 38, 39, 40, 42, 48, 53, 54, 57–62, 65, 71, 73–75, 93, 96, 111
   as process, 38, 48, 53
   non-normative, legitimate, 53
   maternal, 54
atmospheres, 25, 56, 80, 111

B

Barad, Karen, 15
   difference, 15, 45
   memory, 25
   intra-active tendencies, 56
   mattering, 57, 77, 99
   life force, 59
   agency 63
Bauman, Zygmunt
   fluidity, 3, 10
becoming
   cultural of nature, 4
   relation, 14, 102, 111
   and desire, 54, 111
   as analysis tool, 54–56, 111
   decentered, 111
   as line of flight, 55
   as part of schizoanalysis, 66, 83
   of experience, 76
   as process of differenciation, 83, 107, 111
   as process of transformation, 84, 86
   space, 102
   immanent, 111
becoming-woman
   as claiming identity, becoming minority, 87–88, 111
   as secular, 113
   Also see minority
being, 26, 107, 112
   ways of, 5, 20, 23, 95
   politics of, 19
   modes of, 20
   embodied being, 23
   a woman, 40
   Laestadian, 44
   sexual being, 77
   responsive to the difference, 104
   nomadic ways of, 113
belief, 63, 76
   systems of, 3
   personal, 35
Bergson, Henri
   creative evolution, xiv
   processes, 4
   time, 10
   memory, 25
   affect, 25, 58
   intensities, 71
   movement, 107
   -ian methodology, 4

body/bodies, 14, 23, 25, 53, 55, 56, 62, 66, 71, 75, 76–79, 80, 82, 83, 107, 111
  female body, 12, 81–83
  as site of ethics and knowledge, 21
  of writing, 23
  and affect, 58
  as a living arrangement, 78–81
  machine, 78
  embodied, 3, 7, 15, 22, 23, 80, 111, 112
  bodily, xiii, 23, 42, 63, 71, 76, 100
  mind/body binary, 12
  relation, 12
Braidotti, Rosi, 12, 15, 24, 42, 48, 54, 55, 56, 57, 79, 83
  sustainable ethics, 6, 104
  difference-from, 13
  cartographies, 41
  non-normativity, 53, 99
  machinic, 64, 81
  nomadism, 84
  becoming minority, becoming-woman, 87–88
  differences within, 97

C
cartography, 22, 41, 57
  cartographical lines, 57, 72
  cartographic mappings, 71
Cixous, Hélène, 39, 54
  Écriture feminine, 22–23, 42, 56
  writing on embodied experience, 40
Colebrook, Clare, 12, 54, 56
collective, 12, 14, 22, 23, 42, 48, 59, 60, 74, 75, 80, 82, 100, 111, 112, 113
  inquiry, 6
  biography, 22, 24–25
  writing, 27
  data production, 43, 46, 73, 95, 98, 100
  memories, 45
  practices, 58
  machines of collective desire, 65, 72
  power, 76
  subject, 81
  lines, 83
  methods, 99
constellation
  fluid, processual, xiii, 14, 83, 14
  becoming, 55
  of lines, 57, 84
  collective, 59

  social, 95
  of inquiry, 96
  of subjectivity, 98
  methodological, 102
  of aspiration, 111

D
Davies, Bronwyn, 15, 20, 21, 23, 27, 41, 83
  a body of writing, 23, 39
  collective biography, 25
  writing against the grain, 39
  relationality, 42, 45
  affective intensities, 43
  emergent listening, 43–44
  enlivening of being, 45–46
  feminist poststructuralist methodology, 54, 55
Deleuze, Gilles, 6, 10, 15, 19–21, 41, 48, 76, 93, 100
  differential ontology, 8
  subject and knowledge, 13–14
  memory, 24, 25
  repetition, 26
  event, 28
  schizoanalysis, 53–55, 59–66, 71–87, 112
  becoming and subjectivity, 54–55
  mapping and mattering of lines, 57–58
  desire, 59, 71, 87, 96
  religion, 75
  sexuality, deterritorialization, 78
  process, 99
  experience, 100
  becoming space, 102
  sustainable ethics, 104
Deleuzian, 25
Denzin, Norman, xii, 5, 6, 15, 22, 42
desire, 40, 81, 93
  fluid constellation, xiii
  concept of, 53, 54, 59, 60, 61, 65, 71, 83, 111
  as life force, 59, 60, 63, 64, 87, 111
  schizoanalysis, 60–63, 93, 96
  as force in the intention, 63
  collective desire, 65
  sexual desire, 78
  as machinic arrangement, 78, 87, 112
desiring machines, 60–61, 63–66, 71–72, 74, 77–78, 80, 93, 111, 112
difference, xv–xvi, 11, 4, 14, 15, 45, 60, 73, 99, 106, 107, 111, 112
  possibilities and potentials, 4

politics of, 4
within, 6, 97
and mucosity, 12
difference-from, 13
inequality, oppression, and exclusion based on, 15
constructions of, 15
time and, 15
language and, 21
feminist writing and, 42
and research ethics, 49
between concept and life, 58
production of, 95
and desire, 97
feminist poststructuralist methods and, 97
in (un)producing the same, 100
being responsive to difference, 104
differenciation, 8, 9, 14, 65, 111
processes of, 15
and memory, 26
and becoming, 83
discourse, 5, 8, 12, 20, 41, 86, 100, 106
victimizing, 22, 63, 99
normative, 99, 100
disposition, 55, 72, 79, 111, 112
Dolphijn, Rick, 25

E
ecological
    production, 12
    worlds, 60
    forces, 72
    processes, 87
    system, 103
    approach, 103
ecology, 106, 107, 111
Écriture feminine, 22–23, 42
encounter, xiv, xvi, 9, 11, 21, 27, 38, 42–45, 48, 63, 79, 80, 83, 86, 96, 98, 99, 107, 111
    affective intensity of, 3
    face-to-face, 6, 38, 42, 44, 56
    human and other, 7
    become data, 20
    encounter-production, 25
    immanent, 84
enunciation, 14, 24, 41, 42, 53, 55, 57, 62, 63, 66, 71, 78, 84, 98, 100, 112
    collective, 111

epistemology, 19
    -ical, 7, 8, 22, 35, 49
ethics, 6, 15, 19, 21, 35, 59, 75
    affirmative sustainable, xiii, xvi, 4, 6, 104
    of inquiry, xiii, xv, 4
    humanist, xv, xvi, 12
    -cal perspectives, xv
    situational, xvi, 7, 12, 44, 103, 104
    ethico-aesthetics, theory, 12
    of event, 44
    of feminist critical poststructuralist inquiry, 6, 21, 23, 46–48, 107
    of collaborative work, 46
    Spinoza's naturalistic, 58
    personal, 76
    and fluid methodologies, 104
Ettinger, Bracha, L., 22, 54, 63
    co-encounter, 45–46
    matrixial transsubjectivity, 81, 83
event, xiv, xvi, 3, 5–9, 11, 19, 20, 24–28, 38, 41–45, 48, 55–57, 60, 66, 71, 73, 82, 84, 96, 98, 101, 111, 113
eventhood, 7
experience, 13, 14, 21, 24, 25, 42–46, 56, 58, 71, 74, 96, 100
    human(ist), 3, 19, 99
    intensity of, 3
    lived, 12, 21
    past in, 15
    marginalized, 21
    subjective, 24
    collaborative writing, shared, 27
    embodied, 39, 40
    personal, 45, 59
    intensity and, 44, 72, 98
    knowledge and, 46
    immediate, becoming of, 76
    voiced, 98
    of minority, 111

F
faith, xiii, 37, 55, 59, 74–75, 77, 81, 86, 96, 112
    desiring machines of, 65
    processes of, 72
feeling, 25, 40, 43, 45, 82, 111
    thinking and, 59, 76
    emotion, 56

female, 79
  body, 12, 81
  writing, 22, 56
  authorship, 23
  femaleness and sexuality, 36
  to claim identity, 38
  desiring machines of subjectivity, 65, 72
  subject, 82, 84–86
  norm, 83
  model, 85
  empirical, 88
  post, gender, 103
feminist
  poststructuralist approach, xiii, xiv, xv, 21
  (poststructuralist) methodologies, xiii, xvi, 9, 12, 15, 19, 22, 33, 46, 54, 55, 95, 107
  (poststructuralist) inquiry, xv, 5, 6, 19, 20, 23, 35, 46, 47
  critical social inquiry, 6, 93, 107
  (poststructuralist theory), 11, 12, 13, 20, 21, 22, 54, 55, 56
  postcolonial theories, 13, 54
  discourse, 13, 36
  vision, objectivity, 14, 21, 45
  (poststructuralist) methods, 15, 19, 23, 46, 97
  writing practice, 22, 27, 42
  ethnography, 35
  research ethics, 47, 101, 107
fluidity
  of inquiry, xiv–xvi, 9, 20, 97, 103, 106
  concept of, xiii, 3, 10, 11, 12, 14, 93
  of time, 15
  in data production, 28
  and movement, 101, 104
  in critical qualitative research, methodologies, as methodological space, 101–102
  as force, 104, 105
fold
  enfoldings, 25
  processes of (un)folding, 63
  (un)foldings, xiv, xvi, 66, 71, 81, 86, 111
  (un)foldings of subjectivity, 72
force, 3, 8, 12, 56, 57, 78, 79, 80, 84, 104, 112
  of expression, 3, 58
  normative, 20
  subjugating, 22
  sexual, 36, 78
  aspirational, 57, 62
  and faith, 59, 74
  -feel, 59, 104
  life force, 59, 104
  machinic, 60, 78, 79, 81, 112
  social, 60, 72
  desire, 62–64, 78, 87, 96, 111
  personal, 72
  ecological, 72
  arrangement of, 78
  and body, 79, 80, 81
  becoming of, 83–84
  immanent, 87, 112
  fluidity, 93, 104, 105
  affective, 104
  differenciation, 111
  transcendental, 112
  lines, 112
  molar, 76
Foucault, Michel
  subjectification, 12, 54
  knowledgeable subject, 13
  ethics of schizoanalysis, 99

G

Gannon, Susanne, 23, 27
  collective biography, 25
  relationality, 42, 45
  enlivening of being, 45–46
  feminist poststructuralist methodology, 54
gender
  as a fluid constellation, xiii
  identities, 6, 39
  as process, 8
  constructions, 13
  differences, 15, oppression, 21, 103
  -ed narratives, 39
  female, 48
  temporary formations of, 53
  fluid constellations of, 83
  post, 102
  performed, 102
  as difference, 106
Grosz, Elizabeth
  difference, 15
  memory and time, 25
  becoming, 84, 96
Guattari, Félix, 6, 21, 41, 48
  ethico-aesthetics, theory,12
  three ecologies, 14, 86

expression, 14
schizoanalysis, 53–55, 59–66, 71–87, 112
   becoming and subjectivity, 54–55
   mapping and mattering of lines, 57
   modalizations of subjectivity, 57
   desire, 59, 71, 87, 96
   religion, 75
   sexuality, deterritorialization, 78

H

Haraway, Donna J., 10
   sustainable ethics, xvi
   situated knowledges, 14, 35, 41, 46, 59, 100, 102
   making kin with the world, 107
Haug, Frigga
   memory-work practice, 24–25, 42
   co-researching, 46–47
Hickey-Moody, Anna, 53, 85
human, 25, 47, 60, 96, 99, 100, 111, 112
   (-ist) subject, xiv, xv, 21, 23, 64, 87
   (-ist) ethics, xvi, 12
   experience, 3, 19
   processes, 7
   encounters, 111
   conditions, 8
   other-than-, non-human, 14, 99, 111
   western male, 22
   body, 25, 78
   rights issue, 36
   desire, 87
   affect and, 111
   posthumanist, 111

I

identity, xiii, 8, 37, 39, 44, 54, 55, 59, 74
   categories of, 13
   constructions of, 22, formation processes, 22, 54
   maternal, 36
   female, 38
   claiming, 87, 113
   constellations of, 98
immanent, 112
   processes, 4, past/future, 26
   planes of compositions, 27
   arrangement, 78
   body, 78
   encounter, 84
   force, 87
   productions, 100
   immanence, 44
inequality 9, 15
   inequity, 4, 5, 102, 103
   equality, xv
intensity, xiii–xvi, 4–6, 9, 19, 25, 41–44, 56–59, 62, 71–73, 80, 84, 86, 93, 95, 98, 107, 111, 112
   affective, 3
intensification 12
Irigaray, Luce
   female body speficity, 11, 81
   feminist writing, 22
   feminist (poststructuralist) theory, 54, 55, 56

J

K

knowledge, xv, xvi, 47, 102, 105
   production, 3, 6
   situated knowledges of (feminist postructuralist) inquiry, 5, 10, 11, 13, 14, 21, 22, 35, 46, 102
   minority, decentered, 7, 14, 111
   from singular to compound, 9
   -in-the-making, formation processes, 10, 14, 42, 99, 101, 106
   absolute, 19
   individual, 21
   -making practices, 21
   ethics of, 21
   through embodied writing, 23
   practices of construction, 42
   validity of, 99
   humanist, 100
   difference and, 100
   -able subject, 13
Koro-Ljungberg, Mirka, xiv, 3, 7–10, 27, 93, 97, 99, 100–106
Kristeva, Julia
   feminist writing and theory, 22, 56

L

Laestadianism, 35–37, 54, 77, 84
Laestadian movement, 35, 36, 39, 46
   community, 38, 47–48, 55, 60, 73, 75, 78–82, 84–87

Laestadius, Lars Levi, 35
Lather, Patty, 14, 15, 20
    feminist poststructuralist research methodology, 19, 21–22, 54
    feminist research ethics, 47
    poststructuralist analysis, 96, 98–99
lines, 59–60, 71
    non-normative, 7, 22
    of inquiry, 7
    narrative, 8, 98
    of expression, 41
    in schizoanalysis, 53, 60–66
    becoming and, 55
    arrangement of, 57, 65, 66, 71, 75, 79, 84
    mapping of, movement of, 57, 71–73
    analysis of story-, 74–88, 96, 98, 107
    molar, 75, 77
    nomadic, 84, 87
    molecular, 112

M

machines
    for analysis, 54
    molecular, 60
    sub-, 72, 87
    Also see desiring machines
machinic, 64, 81
    force, 60, 78, 79
    productions, 60
    arrangements, 62, 78
    in formations, resonances and vibrations, 64
    in the body, 79–80
    energy, 80
    in collective subject, 81
    desiring machines, 112
MacLure, Maggie, xiv, 28, 45, 56, 97, 99, 100
Mahmood, Saba
    feminist postcolonial theory, 36, 53, 54, 88
Malins, Peta, 53, 85
Manning, Erin, xvi
    philosophical exploration, 3
    movement, expression, 14
    thought in the act, 20
    language and movement, 41
    singular and plural, 84
    knowledge, 106
    politics of touch, sensing, 107
mapping, 12, 24, 41–42, 53, 57, 62, 66, 71, 98, 113

marginal, 4, 6, 19, 21, 22, 23, 85, 111
Massumi, Brian
    philosophical exploration, 3, 58
    process ontology, affirmative methodology, 4, 7
    time, temporality, moment, event, 8, 10, 28, 41, 42, 57
    thought in the act, 20
    affect and memory, 25
    language and movement, 41
    affect, intensities, 58, 71
    schizoanalysis, 60
    exemplary method, 91
memory, 24–26, 42, 82
    work, xv, 24–25, 46
    reminiscence, 26
    re-membering, 26
Minh-ha, Trinh, 15
    feminist postcolonial theory, 54
minority, 7, 87, 97, 99, 100
    knowledges, 14, 19
    aspirations, 54
    desiring machines of, 72
    position, 87
    becoming, becoming-woman, decentered becoming, 87, 111, 113
Mohanty, Chandra T., 13
    feminist postcolonial theory, 54
    differences within, 97
molar
    lines, 75, 77, 112
    forces, 76
    strata, 79
    structures, 85, 87
    arrangement, 86
    constructions, 112
    aggregates, 112
molecular, 104
    machines, 60
    arrangement, 86
    lines, 112
    packs, collectives, 112
motherhood, 36, 37, 40, 54, 83
    Laestadian, 37, 54
    desiring machines of motherhood, mothering, 65, 72, 80
motion
    methodologies in, xvi, 4, 93
    fluidity and, 10
    -nal, 41

Index

non-linear, 96
movement, 53, 56, 64
    in methodology, xiii–xv, 3–6, 8, 9, 15, 93, 101, 104, 106
    creative, xiv
    of inquiry, xvi, 6, 95
    in data, xv, 53–56, 59, 61–63, 71–73, 98
    of time, 8, 9
    within female body specificity, 11–12
    fluidity and, 14, 93, 101, 104
    difference and, 15
    in writing, 23
    memory, time and, 25–28
    language, event and, 41, 96
    and becoming, transformational, 55
    non-linear, of intensities, 56
    narrative, 57
    mapping of, 57
    affective, 59
    differenciation and, 65
    of lines, 53, 66, 71, 72, 75, 77, 80, 84, 86, 87
    of forces, 79
    of affection, 79
    of reflection, 96
    transculturation-in-, emergent, life as, inverse, 107
    dispositions and, 112
    Also see Laestadianism
mucosity (mucous), 11–12

N

narrative, 5, 23, 24, 27, 42–44, 66, 98
    creations, counter-, 7
    lines, 8
    meta-, 20, 100
    cultural, 20, 21
    of body, 23
    as embodied self-expression, 42
    processes, personal, 24
    gendered, 39
    form, 56
    movement, 57
    humanist, 99

O

open-endedness, viii, xv, 4, 5, 7, 11, 15, 19, 42, 48, 54, 73, 93, 96, 97, 98, 99, 100,
oppression, 4, 5, 7, 13, 15, 21, 102, 103, 111

P

Pisters, Patricia
    non-normativity, 53, 99
politics
    of future, 4
    of difference, 4
    of life examination, 5, 107
    local, 6
    of being, 19, transformational, 36
    inclusive, 36
    of Laestadian movement, 36–38
    emancipatory, 100
    of touch and sensing, 107
    of life, 107
postcolonial feminist theories, 13, 54
postmethodology, 3, 101
poststructuralist
    approach, xiii, xiv
    inquiry, 23
    methodologies, xv, xvi, 5, 15, 33, 95
    theories, 20, 21
    analysis, 53, 96
potential, 4, 22, 28, 53, 57, 71, 93, 95, 106
potentiality, 56
power, 5
    oppressive, xvi, 5
    structures of, 5, 46
    discourses of, 5, 23
    knowledge and, 8
    means of, 21
    relations, 21
    in research, 35, 46, 47, 100
    formations of, 57
    labor, 60
    religious, 75, 112
    collective, 76
    patriarchal, 87
    human centered, 96
    decentered becoming and, 111
process
    of data production, xiii, xvi, 33, 99, 100
    of life, xiii, 11, 14, 21
    of inquiry, xiii, xiv, 5, 11, 12, 19, 20, 95–97, 107
    methodological, 8, 9, 49
    living and non-living, other-than-human and non-human, 14
    of differenciation, 15, 83
    Also see religious processes
    Also see aspirational processes

Also see identity formation processes
Also see processes of becoming
Also see ecological processes
Also see processes of knowledge formation
Also see affective processes

Q

R
relationality, 45, 59, 87
relational, 4, 7, 45, 59, 74, 83, 97, 106, 111
religion, 55, 60, 86, 87, 112
    desiring machine of, 65, 75
    desire production, 87
religiousness, 87
religious processes, 38
reproduction, 37, 54
reproductive rights, 36

S
schizomethodology, 61
schizoanalysis, 53–54, 60–62, 64, 65–66, 71–72, 111
self
    as a process, 14,
    -justification, 22
    -documentation, 22
    -expression, 23, 42
    embodied, 23
    formation of, 24
    self-esteem, 44
    -constitution, 54
    as threshold, 54
    -explanatory movement, 96
sexuality, 77–80
    female, 36
    desiring machines of, 65, 72
situatedness
    of research, xv, 5, 8, 10, 20, 57, 59
    of concepts, 6
    of feminist inquiry, 19
    of language, 21
    of researcher, 35
    fluidity and, 103
    situational ethics, 7, 12, 44
social
    critical social inquiry, xii, xv, xvi, 4, 5, 6, 14, 42

injustices, 5
change, 7, 35
justice, 7, 101
conditions, 8
production, 12, 63, 75, 81
constructions, 13, 20
norms, 37
processes, 38, 62, 74
formations, 57
forces, 60, 72
society, xiii, 21, 24, 55, 60, 85–87
socius, 86
societal
    tasks, 6
    norms, 40
    analysis, 60
    discourses, 100
    climate, 105
socio-symbolic, 88
    -political, 8, 9, 103, 105
    -cultural-political, 105
spacetime, 10, 14, 45
space-time-matter, 25
    mattering, 6, 25, 42, 56, 57, 59
spatial
    conditions, 9
    processes, 10
    information, 66
Spinoza, Baruch
    affect, 25
    naturalistic ethics, 58
Spivak, Gayatri, 14, 53, 100
    feminist postcolonial theory, 54
    differences within, 97
Stengers, Isabelle, xvi
St. Pierre, Elizabeth A., 5, 99
    feminist poststructuralist inquiry, 19, 20, 23
    writing as method, 27
    nomadic inquiry, 48
stratum, 78
    strata, 79
subject, 12–15, 20, 21, 54, 78, 87, 111, 113
    humanist, xvi, xv, 64
    category of, knowledgeable, 13
    speaking, 14
    individual, 15, 98
    human, 22
    western white male, 22, 23
    agentic, 23

Index

experience in the, 24
of research, study, 47, 97
as abstraction, 55
collective, 81
female, 82, 84–86
as constellation, 98
subject-object, 8, 12, 24
subjectivity, 13, 20, 24, 54, 55, 111–113
   modalities of, 3, 14, 15, 55, 66, 71, 98, 112
   processes of, 12, 113
   analysis of, 13
   formations of, 37, 112
   aspirations and, 53, 71
   modelizations of, 57
   desired, 57, 83
   machinic and, 64
   nomadic, 65
   unfoldings of, female, 72
   formation process, 72, 112
   co-constitution of, 83
   constellations of, 83, 98
   becoming of, 111
   Also see articulation
   Also see disposition

T
time, 8–10, 20, 26
   -line, 107
   -ly synchronized, 27
   timespaces, 23
   duration of, 26
temporal
   engagement, 3
   process, 10
   arrangement, 60, 96
   explorations, 93
   -ity, 10, 20
transcendent, 78, 112
   transcendental, 86, 112

U

V
van der Tuin, Iris, 23, 25
voice
   of speaking subject, 14

in text, 23
of minority, 23, 99
and agency, 98

W
Whitehead, Alfred N.,
   process ontology, 8
   affect, 58, 59
   becoming of experience, 76–77
womanhood, 36, 40, 41, 48, 86, 111
   Laestadian, 37
   desiring machines of, 65, 72
writing, xiv, 3, 43, 48
   collaborative, xv, 27, 46, 71, 98
   autobiographical, 15, 22–23, 38, 40–41, 55- 56, 71
   act of, 22, 24, 27
   as feminist practice, 22, 42
   as emancipatory practice, 22
   body of writing, 23
   collective writing, 27
   writing assignment, 38–39, 42, 44
   process of, 27, 39, 42
   experience of, 39, 46

X

Y

Z